ACHIEVING AGAINST THE ODDS

African American Professional Women in Higher Education

Anita P. Jackson, Ph.D. and Marlene R. Dorsey, Ph.D.

AuthorHouse™
1663 Liberty Drive
Bloomington, IN 47403
www.authorhouse.com
Phone: 1-800-839-8640

First published by AuthorHouse 6/29/2009

ISBN: 978-1-4343-7706-7 (sc)

Printed in the United States of America
Bloomington, Indiana

This book is printed on acid-free paper.

Dedication

*To African American Ph.D.'s everywhere,
who are toiling in the halls of academia*

Acknowledgements

To the gracious and phenomenal women who participated in this study

To our families who encouraged and inspired us along the way

To those who have supported us and who love us

CONTENTS

Foreword

It is a well-known fact that African American women with doctoral degrees in the United States comprise only a miniscule percentage of the overall number of faculty members and administrators working at institutions of higher learning. What are perhaps much less well-known and understood, however, are the numerous challenges that African American women continue to face in the contemporary period as well as the various strategies and coping mechanisms they utilize to achieve success within the ivory towers of academia. It is in this area that *Achieving Against the Odds: African American Professional Women in Higher Education* by Drs. Anita P. Jackson and Marlene R. Dorsey makes a refreshingly original, notable, and significant contribution.

This work is written in the historical backdrop of a number of major events and factors that have greatly impacted not only Black women's involvement in higher education in recent decades, but also that of Black men. These factors are numerous and varied, including the famous *Brown vs. the Board of Education* ruling in 1954, which successfully decimated the principle of "separate but equal"; the monumental Civil Rights Act of 1964; the subsequent affirmative action legislation that was passed to "level the playing field" for various racial and gender groups in this country; and the increasing number of African American women who have enrolled in recent decades at both Black and White educational facilities for higher education.

The authors skillfully remind us that even though there has been an increase in the number of African Americans who have received doctoral degrees over the past thirty years, there is still a very large under-representation of African American faculty members, both male and female, comprising a meager 3 percent of all faculty members at these institutes of higher learning. Moreover, when African American faculty members do work at these various educational institutions, they tend to form the base rather than the apex of the academic pyramid of influence, prestige, and power. In other words, the vast majority of African Americans (male and female) still tend to be concentrated at the lowest academic rank as assistant professors, with very few being elevated to the highest rank in academia: full professorship.

Black women's "invisibility" in the ivory towers of academia has many notable impacts. As Patricia Hills Collins has so eloquently argued, "Black women's exclusion from positions of power within mainstream institutions has led to the elevation of elite White male ideas and interests and the corresponding suppression of Black women's ideas and interests in traditional scholarship. Moreover, this historical exclusion means that stereotypical images of Black women permeate popular culture and public policy."[1]

Within this context, *Achieving Against the Odds* becomes even more relevant for interpreting Black women's struggles and triumphs in the 21st century political economy in the United States because the authors place Black women at the center rather than the periphery of their analysis. Thus, in a sense, the authors privilege African American women's voices. They provide us with a marvelous birds-eye-view of the inner lives, activities, and coping strategies of five successful African American women administrators who hold the position of dean or the rank of either associate or full professor at predominantly White institutions of higher learning. These women's uniqueness lies in the fact that they have been able to succeed in spite of the numerous obstacles placed before them. *Achieving Against the Odds* thus becomes a wonderful exposition of the possible rather than the impossible by sharply illuminating the paths, trajectories, and strategies that these women have used to enhance their own survival in different university settings, geographical areas, and

1 Patricia Hill Collins, (2000). Black feminist thought: Knowledge, consciousness, and the politics of empowerment, 2nd Edition. New York: Routledge Chapman and Hall, p. 5.

family situations. Now that they have created their own paths and trajectories for success, it is my hope that many other women will follow.

From a methodological perspective, the authors utilized a holistic approach to understanding human behavior by looking at the five women not in virtual isolation from each other, but as individuals who were connected across time and space by virtue of a number of important factors and commonalities, including their historical links to Africa and their reliance and emphasis on the importance of utilizing their extended family networks, deep-seated spiritual values, and desire to succeed in spite of the odds. To assist them in making these important connections, the authors presented various types of data to substantiate their arguments while interweaving rich and vibrant life histories and oral narratives of the five women who form the focus of this book. Drs. Jackson and Dorsey are successful in utilizing the Nguzo Saba approach as outlined some years ago by Dr. Maulana Karenga. The Nguzo Saba approach relies on the use of seven important principles of living: umoja—unity; kujichagulia—self-determination; ujima—collective work and responsibility; ujamaa—cooperative economics; nia—purpose; kuumba—creativity; and imani—faith. These seven principles are discussed and interwoven throughout the book as they apply to specific strategies utilized by the five women in this study to build productive lives and achieve success in higher education.

Achieving Against the Odds is an academic *tour de force* that makes a powerful and lasting contribution to the fields of African American Studies, Women's Studies, and Sociology. The study's findings make us keenly aware of one irrefutable fact: the recruitment, hiring, and subsequent movement of Black faculty and administrators throughout the academic hierarchies of predominantly White institutions of higher learning is inexorably interwoven with these same universities' efforts to successfully recruit, retain, and graduate minority students through the implementation of various diversity programs. One recruitment cannot succeed without the other. Drs. Jackson and Dorsey bring a high level of authenticity to their research and analysis of this issue, which is to some extent reflective of the fact that these two Black women are both successful faculty members and administrators at the same type of institutions about which they write. They have already experienced many of the same challenges and struggles articulated by the five Black successful female academicians who are the main focus of their book. I would strongly recommend this book to anyone who is interested in knowing more about the Black woman's experience in America. This book is particularly useful to students, academics, administrators of higher education, and members of the public at large.

Dr. Bessie House-Soremekun
Public Scholar in African American Studies, Civic Engagement, and Entrepreneurship
Professor of Political Science
Professor of African American and African Diaspora Studies
Indiana University Purdue University in Indianapolis (IUPUI)

INTRODUCTION

> Girl, it's 11:30. Why are we still sittin' up here in this office? You know we should both be home gettin' some sleep. It's gonna be daylight before you know it.
>
> Yeah! But when else are we going to get to talk, just the two of us, about *real* things without interruptions and without having to run around here like chickens with our heads cut off? When else are we going to get our work completed?

Thus begins our story of the lives of African American women with PhDs traversing the halls of academia as administrators and faculty, women who, through their dedication and perseverance, have carved out their place in what has traditionally been foreign territory. *Achieving Against the Odds: African American Professional Women in Higher Education* recounts the success stories of five African American women administrators and faculty members in predominantly White institutions of higher education (PWIs). More specifically, these are administrators who hold upper echelon administrative positions or are tenured faculty with a position above the level of assistant professor. They have made it past the academy's "gate-keepers" and moved on to receive status and rewards that have been traditionally reserved for White men. These five women have achieved at a high level and are, by institutional standards, successful. Achieving at this level is quite an accomplishment in view of the fact that African American women are relatively new to White academia and still encounter many forms of bias and oppression (see Alfred, 2001; Antonio, 2002; Bradley and Holcomb-McCoy, 2004; Gregory, 1995).

Achieving Against the Odds began evolving several years ago in informal conversations with African American women who expressed their joys, disappointments, successes, and struggles in the academic setting. These discussions, as well as our own personal experiences and observations, brought into sharp focus the unique challenges and various forms of oppression that exist in the university setting. Although academia is an environment of intellectual investigation and is considered as exemplifying open-mindedness, African American women still speak of the oppressive conditions they endure that are unique to them. As a result of these conditions, many become disheartened by the experience and some decide to leave the academy. Some stay but are unable to advance their position. Others, for a variety of reasons, decide to stay and manage to do exceptionally well. The questions posed in this writing center on those who have succeeded. We ask: "How and why are some African American women able to continue and succeed in academia? What personal and professional fulfillment do African American women obtain working in a PWI? How do African American administrators and faculty negotiate the demeaning, oppressive, and often exclusionary practices of the university? These are our most pressing questions.

The literature (Alfred, 2001; Antonio, 2002; Bradley and Holcomb-McCoy, 2004; Gregory, 1995, 2001; etc.) attests to the obstacles African American women encounter in academia and the negative impact of these roadblocks. While there is some research on African American faculty in predominantly White institutions (Aguirre, 2000; Alfred, 2001; Bradley and Holcomb-McCoy, 2004; Cooper, 2006; Gregory, 1995, 2001; Smith, Wolf, and Busenberg, 1996; Thomas and Hollenshead, 2001; Turner and Myers, 2000), a paucity of research exists on African American faculty and administrators who have endured and succeeded in such institutions. Therefore, we feel that it is important to capture the experiences and perspectives that have enabled these successful women to reach the heights of their profession. If we understand how African American women succeed in academia, despite the obstacles they face, we can provide a pathway to success for those who follow. We can implement strategies that will enable the academic environment to be more conducive to the gifts and talents that African American women bring.

We feel honored to be investigating this area of research as too often the voices of African American women are ignored or silenced. Research on gender and race has historically ignored the unique perspectives of African American women. Therefore, we are especially interested in the observations, reflections, and strategies of African American women as administrators and faculty regarding their personal journeys of success and achievement. We want to hear the stories of how they have confronted, managed, and overcome obstacles. We have implemented a qualitative investigation to identify common themes in the experiences of these African American women administrators and faculty. In essence, our investigation is an attempt to give voice to their survival and success in the academy.

Another reason has compelled us to do this research. We are troubled by the relentless barrage of negative images and stereotypes of African American women that abound in the media, research, and even in literary works. We have been reminded over and over again that "there is a problem in Black America." We are all too familiar with the stories on poverty, crime, drug abuse, teenage pregnancy, high school drop-out rates, and high college attrition rates. Even now, when there is good news to report about Black college attendance (especially among young women), we nevertheless manage to get consistently assaulted with negative images and bizarre tales of inability to handle pressure, lack of motivation, and the bell-curve theory as evidence of intellectual inferiority. Unfortunately, many of the stereotypes specific to African American women (matriarch, superwoman, etc.) established during the period of enslavement have persisted in the general population up to the present. Such stereotypes adversely affect the perception that those in academia have about African American administrators and faculty. A focus on successful African American administrators and faculty can assist in changing such perceptions.

Certainly, African American communities are not without their issues. While problems exist, there are also many success stories to tell. There are positive images to celebrate and role models to emulate, and a number of these can be found in the academy. We believe that these stories must be told. We also believe that these stories should be told from an Afrocentric paradigm. Gregory (1995, 2001) noted that traditional studies by social scientists have been based on stereotypes and misconceptions. Akbar (1984) recognized that traditional, Eurocentric research paradigms have served the function of perpetuating oppression and erroneously depicting the reality of the victims of oppression. In the past 30–40 years alone, African American scholars such as Billingsley, Hill, Nobles, Staples, Walker, and Willie, have sought to challenge stereotypes that have served to negatively characterize African American women and ignore the strength of their passion for survival and achievement (Gregory, 1995). Akbar (1984) argued that the paradigm of African American research must depict the best of human development. Other researchers (Davis, 1983; Lipford-Sanders and Bradley, 2005; Rothenberg, 1998; Williams, 2005) have noted also the importance of contextualizing studies about African Americans within the categories of gender, race, ethnicity, and social class and of noting how these categories impact African American women. These researchers believe that doing so provides a more positive and holistic view of African American women. We agree. Our objective is to hear the voices of the women and to challenge the long history of stereotypical perceptions related to African American women. We want to see a shift from an oppressive negative-image paradigm to a resilient, decidedly positive image paradigm, focusing specifically on African American women in the academy. Thus we have seized the opportunity to tell the success stories of five phenomenal professional women in academia who demonstrate what is possible. **If we intend to attract African American women to careers in the academy, then successful African American women in academia must be showcased.**

We use the Nguzo Saba approach to share the lives of the five African American women in our study. Nguzo Saba refers to seven principles of living, articulated by Dr. Maulana Karenga (1998). The seven principles are unity: umoja—unity; kujichagulia—self-determination; ujima—collective work and responsibility; ujamaa—cooperative economics; nia—purpose; kuumba—creativity; and imani—faith. We discuss the perspectives of the five women and our findings within the context of these seven principles because they represent those qualities that are necessary for positive development, achievement, and success.

CHAPTER 1
Umoja
Connections with Our Collective Past

The hand of a child cannot reach the shelf, nor can the hand of an adult get through the neck of a gourd. (African proverb)

We truly need each other. Despite the traditional emphasis on individualism in our society, connection with our fellow human being is vital. Through connection we can support each other in our development and in our struggle to survive and excel. Through connection we can find common areas of struggle and survival, areas that can unify both our identity and our efforts. Our connection to the past contextualizes current issues and struggles, providing insight necessary for understanding our current place in time and for undertaking unified efforts on current and future initiatives. Examining past concerns, challenges, coping strategies, and remedies reveals a more holistic perspective of our current experiences. Identifying and understanding common areas of struggle and survival among African American women administrators and faculty in academia may facilitate a sense of connection with an ongoing effort. This, in turn, facilitates a sense of sisterhood and unity, as well as future direction and clarity.

In the context of this chapter, unity (umoja) is viewed as a connection with our ancestors as well as with our contemporaries. Therefore, before presenting the findings about the women of this study and their common themes of struggle, survival, and success, we have chosen to begin our story with a brief overview of the history of African American women in the academy, including insights about challenges they face in PWIs.

History of African American Women in the American Academy: Issues and Challenges

African American women have a rich tradition of employment in education and have participated in higher education in the U.S. for well over a century. Many have sought careers in the teaching profession because of their desire to make a difference in the lives of others. Education in the African American community has historically served as a vehicle to escape poverty and to prepare the next generation for leadership. As educators, African American women serve as role models, giving promise to future leaders. They are visible evidence that African Americans can succeed.

While African American women have served in higher education for many years, their presence in predominantly White universities has a relatively short history. Until the 1950s, 96% of all full-time African American faculty were employed by historically Black colleges and universities (Thomas, 1981). More recently, the total number of full-time African American faculty employed at Black colleges was fewer than 45% (Smith, 1992). After the *Brown vs. Topeka, Kansas* desegregation of schools decision in 1954 and the *Civil Rights Act* of 1964, more African American women have been hired as faculty at PWIs. Nevertheless, they are dramatically under-represented. What is worse, during the past four decades their numbers at all institutions of higher education have actually declined. Between 1975 and 1986, the percentages of African American women faculty declined from 4.6% to 3.6% (Gregory, 1995). In 1985, they represented only 1.9% of full-time faculty; 0.6% of full professors, 1.4% of associate professors, 2.7% of assistant professors, and 3% of instructors, lecturers, and other faculty (James and Farmer,

1993). By 1987, African American women faculty represented only 2% of faculty in all institutions of higher education, with only half of those in predominantly White institutions (Snyder, 1987). By 1992, African American women represented 2.3% of higher education faculty and by 1999, slightly under 3%. Even showing a slight increase, the numbers remain small compared to White faculty and other faculty of color (Cooper, 2006). West (1993) stated that never before in the history of education has there been such a myriad of African American intellectuals. There has been an upward trend of African Americans obtaining doctoral degrees over the past 20 years (St. John, 2000), yet universities continue to struggle with under-representation of African American faculty. African Americans, both men and women, represent less than 3% of all faculty (Antonio, 2002; Cooper, 2006).

Additionally, where they are found, they tend to be concentrated among the lower ranks (instructor and assistant professor) and are promoted at a slower rate than their White counterparts. Furthermore, they are generally located in traditional disciplines (education and social sciences), are primarily employed by community colleges, and are paid less than their male and White female counterparts (Brown, 1988; Reskin and Phipps, 1988).

The development of future African American leaders is placed in jeopardy if African American faculty role models are scarcely present in the academy. DeFour and Hirsch (1990) found that the mere presence of Black faculty on campus provides evidence to minority students that they too can complete their education and become competent and successful professionals. Blackwell (1983) found that the number of Black faculty at a college or university is the most important predictor of the first year Black student enrollment, as well as of the retention and graduation rates. Unfortunately, universities are currently experiencing a decline in the number of African American faculty. With affirmative action losing support and efforts to achieve diversity and equity in higher education being contested (Antonio, 2002; Turner, 2002), this decline is likely to continue.

Research also suggests (Gregory, 1995) that the status of African American women as administrators is not impressive. For example, in 1985 only 3.4% of administrators were Black women compared to 30.4% of administrators being White women. The majority of African American administrators were employed at historically Black institutions and were primarily concentrated in student affairs and specialized positions. Like African American women faculty, African American women administrators tend to be older, married, concentrated in two-year institutions, and paid approximately 15% less than their male counterparts (Moses, 1989). African American women represent 3.4% of the total number of administrators in higher education. Most of those women are on primarily Black campuses and concentrated in lower echelon administrative positions (James and Farmer, 1993). This information illustrates not only the under-representation of African American women in PWIs but also speaks to the lack of institutional power they have wherever they are located.

Challenges

In the professional domain, African American women have some of the same concerns as non-African American women. These include pay equity, earning tenure and promotion, juggling family and professional responsibilities, gaining respect as professionals, and exercising power in an environment dominated by men. Beyond these shared concerns, there are issues specific to African American women. These include ideologies and assumptions (stereotypes) about African American women that arose from enslavement experiences and were intended to control and to dominate these women (Bryant, etc., 2005; Reid-Merritt, 1996). The continuation of such ideologies and assumptions promotes racial discrimination, role conflict that is compounded by race, and misperceptions of culturally specific behaviors.

Ideologies and Assumptions

Stereotypes about African American women abound. Stereotypical portrayals of African American women include the matriarch, superwoman, angry Black woman, intellectual inferiority, unattractiveness, and sexual promiscuity. The matriarch cares for everyone. She is faithful, obedient, nurturing, and there for everyone regardless of her own needs. The superwoman is able to do all things. She is able to demonstrate resilience and provide an answer to every problem, whether or not she has the support or resources necessary to achieve the solution. Of course, the angry Black woman is uncooperative, "bitchy", and certainly not well-respected. She is a complainer and has no legitimate issues worth consideration. African American women, as all African American people, have been assumed to have low intellectual abilities. Myths such as possessing mediocre credentials (Smith, Wolf, and Busenberg, 1996) and being "prime hires" simply because they are minority women are often believed by professionals in the academy. African American women, who cannot meet standards of White beauty, are not viewed as attractive. Research has demonstrated that beauty and attractiveness are related to hiring and promotion practices (Ceridian Connections, 2006; Dipboye, etc., 1977; Shahani-Denning, 2003; Viewzone.com, 2005). Lastly, notions of sexual promiscuity do little to enhance a sense of professional identity and self-efficacy among African American women. These stereotypes exact a heavy toll upon African American women in their attempts to succeed in the workplace and, as we examine here, in academia.

Racial Discrimination

African American women experience racial discrimination because of stereotypes held about them. In her 1989 study, Yolanda Moses found that typical racial discriminatory experiences of African American women administrators and faculty include:

1) "being constantly challenged because she is viewed as other and therefore inferior; (read: non-white and female)
2) a lack of professional support systems; (may be the only Black woman in the department; no visible means of support from colleagues; no institutional network)
3) overscrutinization by peers, superiors, and students; - you're black; you can't be qualified; prove that you are;

4) an unstated requirement to work harder in order to gain recognition and respect;
5) assumptions that her job was acquired through affirmative action and, therefore, that she is unqualified for the position;
6) being tokenized, that is, seen as a symbol of her race rather than as an individual; and
7) being denied access to power structures normally associated with her position (let's set her up for failure is the message here)."

Several researchers (Aguirre, 2000; Gregory, 2001; Thomas and Hollenshead, 2001; Turner and Myers, 2000) have found that a pervasive theme which impedes the recruitment and retention of African American faculty is the unwelcoming work environments that are filled with racial and gender biases. Also, African American faculty report not having the benefit of mentoring and support from colleagues (Turner, Myers, and Creswell, 1999). The absence of validation and acceptance creates a sense of alienation for many African American faculty members (Bradley and Holcomb-McCoy, 2004). Thus, African American women often leave academia due to difficulty in obtaining tenure or promotion (Gregory, 1995), feelings of isolation and alienation, and lack of respect (Davis, 1985). Davis (1985) concluded that Black faculty are less satisfied with their college/university positions than White faculty and that Black faculty perceive themselves to be less respected and to have less certain employment futures than White faculty.

Role Conflict

African American women in academia often find themselves serving as mentor, mother, and counselor in addition to educator for African American students attempting to survive in an environment that is often hostile to them. In addition, they are frequently called upon by colleagues and administrators to assume these same roles. Subordination, nurturance, and constant self-sacrifice are expected of African American women in the performance of their duties

(West, 1995; White, 1999). African American women are viewed as faithful, obedient, and supportive of the goals and ambitions of their White male colleagues. On the other hand they are not perceived as possessing strong needs or desires related to their own professional growth and achievement. This role positioning, the expectation that African American women assume roles in accordance with prevailing stereotypes, can be detrimental to the women's careers.

As Gregory (1995) pointed out in her study, we are aware that traditionally most Black women have shown tremendous resilience and strength in facing life's challenges. This strength has too often been misconstrued and stereotyped through the use of terms such as "matriarch" and "superwoman," both referring to a woman who is long-suffering with limited individual needs. The African American woman who internalizes this depiction of herself may find that she is attempting to assume this mantle of strength when in reality she cannot, and it would be harmful for her if she did assume it. If an African American woman does not accept the role of being all things to all people, she is considered cold, unapproachable, antisocial, and not a team player. If she speaks out against her treatment, then she is viewed as an angry, uncooperative, threatening Black woman. She is seen as a trouble maker or even incompetent because she cannot or will not juggle all the responsibilities thrust upon her.

Too often African American women, in their attempt to dismantle being viewed in such a stereotypical manner, will suppress their opinions and feelings, become silent, and try to act in a manner that is non-threatening and more socially acceptable to White society and colleagues. They may even feel guilty that they are unable to help all those who need their help. The personal costs can be physically, emotionally, psychologically, and spiritually devastating (Coker, 2003; Grier and Cobbs, 1992; Williams, 2001). The African American woman who has the least amount of resources, lowest social status, and remains at the bottom of the socioeconomic scale assumes her role of responsibility with equanimity, but often with considerable cost to her health, emotional well-being, and career advancement.

Cultural Worldviews

Another area of conflict for African American women in PWIs has to do with values reflected in cultural world views. A person's world view constitutes one's psychological orientation in life and determines how an individual thinks, behaves, makes decisions, and defines events (English, 1984). A cultural world view represents the philosophical assumptions that underlie a person's or group's perception of the world and how it operates. Just as individuals, groups, and organizational entities hold particular perspectives about how the world and its people function, academia also maintains a specific perspective according to which it operates. The cultural orientation of academia operates on a system that emphasizes competitiveness, individualism, and dichotomous reasoning (Bennett, 1998). This view of the world acknowledges people and everything in the world as separate from one another. As a result, there is a general lack of cooperative spirit that drives people to compete against one another for resources and rewards. These values are often in conflict with the cultural world view or value system of many African American women. The value system of African American women is likely to emphasize cooperativeness, communalism, and diunital (holistic; incorporating opposites) reasoning that is based in traditional African cosmology and philosophy where everything is interconnected. An Afrocentric world view maintains that community is central. There is no dichotomy between spiritual and material; between past, present and future; and between the individual person and the group.

Maruyama (1978) stated that communication breakdowns occur not because people use different vocabulary or language to discuss the same ideas, but because they use different structures of reasoning that stem from their cultural world views. In this regard, African American women who function with a different world view than what is traditionally found at the university are confronted with misinterpretations of their behavior and intentions. The attempt to integrate their own cultural world view or values into their leadership style, teaching, advising, and mentoring is often challenged. For example, on the one hand it may be exciting and educational to bring oral traditions, rhythmic cultures, song, dance, meditation, storytelling, and an informal, interactive style of teaching into the academic curriculum. On the other hand, it is frustrating that colleagues, and frequently students, do not see these activities as integral to the critical thinking process of pedagogy. Questions of purpose, content, goals, competence, and evaluation leap up.

In academia, where individualism often manifests as a prerequisite for success, pressure exists to abandon a spirit of cooperation and neglect connectedness to community, ancestors, and traditional African cosmology and philosophy. However, some African Americans desire and choose to theorize within their own cultural and traditional wisdom. They choose to implement and integrate their own belief system where knowledge is that deepest reality found between the spiritualized ancestors and the physically living thinkers within the community. Nevertheless, they do so at a cost to themselves. Their proclivity for connection is sometimes viewed with suspicion and misconstrued as lacking the ability to work independently.

These challenges create a difficult, threatening, and oppressive atmosphere. We conclude that the situation for many (perhaps most) African American women in PWIs can best be described as a struggle for survival and identity. In spite of the rather daunting odds and circumstances, some African American women have remained in PWIs and have been able to obtain tenure and promotion and to move up in faculty and administrative positions. Considering such obstacles, we ask the question: How have African American professional women in academia developed effective coping and survival skills for the chronic inequities which are institutionalized on a systematic basis?

Coping Mechanisms of African American Women

A review of the literature on coping mechanisms of African American women illustrates that they have acquired a variety of coping strategies due to their long history of dealing with racism, sexism, and poverty. Coping mechanisms that have been typically described are reliance on support systems such as family, extended family, and "sister friends" (Boyd, 1993; Gregory, 1995); religion or spiritual means; a change in self-perception or perception of the situation; flexible gender role identity (Malveaux, 1984); and an internalization of a comprehensive understanding of the African American ethos that includes external attributions of success and failure (Jackson and Sears, 1992; Young, 1989). The relevance of these coping strategies will become evident as the women's stories unfold.

Success and Job Satisfaction

Webster defines success as "the degree or measure of attaining a desired end ... favorable termination of a venture." As implied in the definition, success is not determined by a set of external criteria, but by each individual's interpretation of something desired. Vaughn (1988) stated that the quality of one's success in life is determined by the meanings assigned to events in the life stages. The desired item or situation has meaning to the individual. Furthermore, the thing desired does not often come without a struggle. It can be said that success is measured by the obstacles individuals overcome while trying to succeed.

Job satisfaction is a measure of the quality of work life. Hanson, Martin, and Tuch (1987) stated that it is important to understand what workers most value in a job and whether the job provides what is most valued. Herzberg (1972) identified five major variables of intrinsic job satisfaction. They are achievement, recognition, the nature of the work, responsibility, and advancement. Extrinsic factors are company policy and administration, supervision, salary, interpersonal relations, and working conditions. The university system defines success based on criteria such as tenure and promotion, recognition and respect given by professional colleagues, and/or the amount of money obtained in grants. Racism and sexism are contradictory to the provisions of respect, recognition, and achievement of career requirements. This results in unfavorable working conditions for individuals who are targets of these social ills. According to most African American women administrators and faculty, racism and sexism are constant realities in their work settings. Considering this, how do African American women acquire satisfaction and success in the context of racism and sexism, and what defines success for them? The stories of the five women in our study reveal their responses to these dilemmas.

African American Women and Research

In examining research relative to African American women, two critical issues stand out. First, African American women are too often discussed either under the category of "Blacks," without distinguishing between men and women, or under the category of "women," without distinguishing between White women and Black women (Cooper, 2006; Graves, 1990; Simms and Malveaux, 1986). Second, when the specific issues of African American women are discussed, they are often stereotypically portrayed. As mentioned previously, on one end of the continuum, the African American woman is described as the epitome of strength, a "superwoman," and as a long-suffering, motherly type with limited individual needs. Furthermore, these qualities are idealized as heroic in European-Americans but are viewed as unfeminine when applied to African American women. At the other end of the continuum, the African American woman is depicted as an uncooperative, loud-mouth complainer or as a seductress, a highly sexual being who is responsible for her exploitation and maltreatment. Neither of these descriptions enhances African American women's sense of well-being (McCray, 1980; Rodgers-Rose and Rodgers, 1985). Somewhere in the middle of these extremes, the African American woman finds herself attempting to establish an identity and to define herself. This study attempts to portray African American women with greater authenticity by considering their unique essence as African Americans and as women and by allowing them to tell their stories from their own perspectives.

Method

Desiring to hear the voices of the women lends itself to a qualitative study. Qualitative methods can be used to uncover and understand what lies behind any phenomenon about which little is yet known as well as to gain novel and fresh slants on that which is already known (Strauss and Corbin, 1990). Research on successful African American women in academia is scarce. Our purpose is to understand more fully what enables these women to become successful in an often oppressive or hostile environment. The type of qualitative research utilized in this study is grounded theory. Grounded theory is a means of building a theory inductively based upon the study of the phenomenon it represents. Through grounded theory, one does not begin with a theory and then prove it, but begins with an area of study and allows what is relevant to emerge (Strauss and Corbin, 1990). In this way, the women's stories are expressed, and what is relevant to the phenomenon of success is allowed to emerge. Storytelling fits well with the African American tradition of oral transmission of information and knowledge and is welcomed in this research project.

Participant Selection

The individuals selected for this study are African American women who are tenured associate professors, full professors, or deans and administrators of their departments. Lacking a data base regarding the representation of such women in the Midwestern states in which this study was conducted, the participants were identified utilizing the sampling strategy of snowballing (Miles and Huberman, 1994; Patton, 1990). Snowballing is a process whereby acquaintances of the researchers in various settings (work, place of worship, sports, etc.) identify information-rich informants for the researchers. Informants are people who have a great deal of knowledge about the research topic because they have experienced it. This procedure has proven suitable for obtaining enough participants for an in-depth study of the questions investigated. Once prospective participants were located, they were contacted and offered the opportunity to participate in the study. Although many women wanted to participate, not all felt they could meet the time commitments due to family, personal, or work related demands at the time of the study. Also, geographic location and scheduling limitations prevented our access to interviewing some women.

The criteria for participation are as follows: 1) African American, 2) female, 3) upper level administrative position or faculty beyond junior level status, and 4) employed at a predominantly White university. Ten women were identified; two were unable to devote time to the study, however, and one did not wish to participate. Two women did not meet the criteria for inclusion. One of these women was an assistant professor and the other was employed at a small community college that has a large percentage of non-White employees. Thus five women met the criteria and were interviewed.

Participants

Pseudonyms are used for the five women that have been interviewed. We have purposely chosen pseudonyms that represent historical African women in leadership roles. These were African women who encountered tremendous odds and are recognized as strong, successful women of their days. The pseudonyms used are Cleopatra, Nandi, Nzingha, Tiye, and Amina. The following paragraph highlights the background of the historic women whose names are used.

Cleopatra *Nandi* *Nzingha* *Tiye* *Amina*

Cleopatra VII (69–30 B.C.) was a queen of Egypt. She was intelligent, witty, and ambitious and she attracted some of the greatest Romans of her day. Her skill in mastering many different languages and African dialects was instrumental in elevating Egypt to world supremacy (Clarke, 1992; World Book Encyclopedia, 1976).

Nandi (1778–1826 A.D.) was the mother of Chaka Khan, the great ruler of Zululand. She helped to mount offensives against the slave trade and the colonial system that followed the death of Queen Nzingha (Clarke, 1992).

Nzingha (1583–1663 A.D.) was an Angolan Queen of Matamba and Ndongo, West Africa. She was cunning and prudent as a warrior queen and astute and successful in consolidating power. Nzingha was of an ethnic group called Jagas. The Jagas were an extremely militant group who formed a human shield against the Portuguese slave traders (Clarke, 1992). Nzingha never accepted the Portuguese's conquest of her country and constantly fought against them (Clarke, 1992). She encouraged the first known stirring of nationalism in West Central Africa with her opposition to European domination (Clarke, 1992).

Tiye (1415–1340 B.C.) was a Nubian Queen of Egypt for half a century, mother of Akhnaton and Tutankhamen, mother-in-law of Nefertiti, and wife of Amenhotep III (Spottswood-Simon, 1992). Her opinions commanded respect and she exerted informed political influences throughout her terms as queen consort and queen mother of the most powerful nation of her day.

Amina was a strong leader and ruled Zaria from 1588 to 1589. She is remembered for her fierce military exploits. She has been described as a brilliant military strategist who won every war she led. She is referred to as "Amina, Yar Bakwa ta san rana" which means "Amina—daughter of Nikatau—a woman as capable as a man" (Budweiser Company).

The women in this study reflect the fierce determination and leadership qualities of these historical personalities. The following is background information regarding the five women who have participated in this study.

Cleopatra was visited at a middle-sized midwestern university where she is a dean of a college and a tenured associate professor. Given the low number of African American women in decision making positions and the reality of power dynamics that consistently work against those trying to do viable work, Cleopatra's voice is significant. Cleopatra lives with her husband and two children.

Nandi was visited at a middle-sized midwestern university where she is a tenured associate professor in the Business Administration program. She represents the only African American woman in her program of that status. As a lone member—who has moved out of the realm of junior faculty but still has yet to realize full professorship -- Nandi's voice is important. Nandi is married to her second husband, and her three children are grown and have families of their own.

Nzingha was visited at a small eastern university where she is a tenured full professor in the Law Department. African American women comprise only 0.6% of full professors (James and Farmer, 1993). The experiences and impressions of a woman who has reached such a rare height must be heard. Nzingha is single, has no children, and lives alone.

Tiye is a tenured associate professor in a Counselor Education program at a middle-sized midwestern university. She is another lone voice who needs to be heard. Tiye is married and has two grown children with families of their own.

Amina is a full professor in the Black Studies Department at a middle-sized midwestern university. She also holds an administrative role as the director of the research unit within the department. She brings a wide variety of perspectives from other institutions (eastern and western U.S.) where she has held professorships. Amina is another "rare occurrence" who brings a special voice to the discussion. Amina is divorced and lives alone.

Researchers

The researchers, who are themselves African American women employed in university settings, do not want to make assumptions based on their own academic experiences. Living lives similar to those of the participants, the authors have attended to the unique aspects of these women and have interviewed friends and colleagues of these women. This strategy of making the familiar strange enhances objectivity. The personal experiences of the researchers, both positive and negative, have initiated this research. Because of their own varying perspectives and concerns about the dynamics in the university setting, the researchers seek to understand how other African American women make sense of their experience of being employed in a predominately White academic setting. The researchers' varying experiences and perspectives are also helpful in checking potential biases and ensuring greater objectivity regarding the data gathered.

Interviews

The procedure used to obtain an understanding of the realities of these women in academia was a semi-structured interview. Informed consent was provided for each participant so that the parameters of the research and potential risks were understood. Data collection involved an informal, two hour interview conducted by the researchers. The interview was semi-structured in that it was not limited to the primary questions but allowed for further probing of responses so that the experiences of these women could be more fully understood. Additional data collection included a one-hour session with a friend of each woman for the purpose of triangulating the data. Triangulating data permits the acquisition of information from various sources in order to insure accuracy and alternative perceptions of participants' information. The interviews were conducted in each woman's office and audio-taped. They were focused on six primary questions:

1. What childhood and early adulthood influences helped you to move in this direction and to survive? Who or what were the influences in childhood and early adulthood that helped to shape your life journey?
2. What has academia been like for you? What were the challenges and opportunities that you have encountered throughout your career in academia?
3. What has enabled you to survive? What were the strategies and resources that you utilized for coping, surviving, and achieving?
4. What has been the significance and meaning of academia in your life? How do you define success?
5. What are your future expectations and challenges?
6. What advice would you give to African American women who desire a career in academia?

The questions asked of each friend of the participants are:

1. What has academia been like for your friend?

2. What do you think were the factors that enabled your friend to choose this life direction?
3. What do you think were factors that enabled your friend to be successful?

Analysis Procedure

The audiotapes were submitted for transcription, and patterns and themes have been identified through discussions between the researchers. Constant comparison, moving back and forth among data sets to identify patterns (Strauss and Corbin, 1990), has been used. An analysis matrix (Miles and Huberman, 1994) was constructed to assist with the comparison process. An analysis matrix or meta-matrix (Miles and Huberman, 1994) is a master chart developed to organize and condense the data. Miles and Huberman (1994) described this meta-matrix as a "juxtaposition—a stacking up—of all the single-case displays on one very large sheet or wall chart which allowed inclusion of all relevant, condensed data" (p. 178). Reading through the interviews, each discrete idea was named. Ideas that seem to represent similar phenomena were grouped together as a way of discovering categories and subcategories. Through an examination of the properties and conditions of each category, patterns were noted. Themes were derived through deciding "what things mean, noting regularities, patterns, explanations, possible configurations, causal flows and propositions" (Miles and Huberman, 1994). Qualitative research validity (Marshall and Rossman, 1999) has been preserved by (1) audio-taping and extensive note taking of participants' responses, (2) verification of authenticity of transcripts by the participants, (3) using direct quotes of the participants to define each category and subcategory to maintain authenticity, and (4) connecting the research findings to theoretical perspectives and quantitative studies.

The following chapters provide a glimpse of the women's childhood, adulthood, and academic employment experiences—as well as their hopes and expectations for the future—through their own voices. Within their stories we discover the factors that contribute to their success in academia and life.

CHAPTER 2
Kujichagulia
The Journey to Academia

A community flourishes and survives only when each member flourishes, bringing forth his or her gifts, living in the full potential of his or her purpose.

Everyone is born with a purpose. The full realization of our purpose comes about through the discovery of our innate gifts, recognized and developed through affirmation by community. Somé (1998) noted that "our own inner authority [purpose, gifts] needs the fuel of external recognition to inspire us to fulfill our life's purpose and until this happens, we wait in paralysis for the redemptive social response that rescues us from the dungeon of anonymity" (p. 27). Community enables us to understand our purpose and to bring forth our gifts. As we come to understand more and more regarding our purpose and our gifts, we can function intentionally and with self-determination (kujichagulia). In the following pages we hear the voices of the study participants as they share stories about the impact of their families and communities during their youth. We see how their experiences provide a springboard for self-determination.

So much of who we are and how we think and behave is shaped during our early childhood years. There is an old saying in the Black community—"You've got your man by five"—which suggests that our adult personalities and behaviors are already shaped by the time we are five years old. Research on early childhood development supports this observation. While individuals certainly have the capacity to change across their entire life span, the experiences of infancy and early childhood have a strong and often lasting effect on adulthood (Skolnick, 1986). An individual's life journey results from the interaction of biological, psychological, social, and historical events as well as the individual's responses to these influences and events. Many people influence our thinking and behavior during those impressionable childhood years. Most of us will remember a relative or close family friend who, in very significant ways, has helped to mold us into the adults that we have eventually become.

In this chapter, we view the socialization processes of the women in this study through their experiences from childhood through early adulthood. In particular, we note racial, gender, and class socialization as processes that affect the way the study participants function and view themselves and their world. Their childhood gives us a glimpse into the direction of their future paths. Through their stories of childhood, we peer into the elements that foster the pursuit and acquisition of their dreams and goals, those elements that propel them into successful adults and professionals.

Cleopatra

Cleopatra spent the first eight years of her life in a culturally diverse neighborhood in a large midwestern city. Living with her parents, siblings, and great-grandmother, Cleopatra's childhood is filled with memorable experiences. The family was very close and engaged in many family oriented activities.

"My great-grandmother lived in the house with us. My grandmother was within walking distance. Cousins and others were not too far away, and we were a small family, but close knit. My great-grandmother was probably one of the greatest influences on me in many ways. I remember so much the closeness of my family. I remember celebrating Christmas and Easter with many family members. Holidays were especially wonderful. Christmas was ... magical. I have many fond memories of childhood."

Cleopatra also speaks of the makeup of the neighborhood and remembers it as a pleasant and satisfying environment. "We lived in what I consider a storybook kind of house. The neighborhood was integrated. There were Whites. There were Italians. There were Blacks. I think for me, interacting with people of different backgrounds was a good thing. The interesting thing is color made no difference, and that was a childhood experience I remember. I liked that part of it."

Church has had a significant impact upon Cleopatra, also. She basically grew up in church. "My mother played the piano in church. My grandmother was a leader in the church and had the title of mother. My great-grandmother was a minister. I spent considerable time in church and found it to be a supportive community. I honed my organizational and communication skills and developed an inner strength in spirituality. Church was a place I could go and know that I would be accepted and nurtured as part of a larger community. It is still a source of strength for me."

Those earlier experiences are quite a contrast from the experiences of Cleopatra when her family moved to another city. The family moved when Cleopatra was about eight years old, and life changed considerably for her in this new urban, predominantly African American environment. Upon first arriving in their new location, the family lived with some cousins until they were able to obtain their own home. Although Cleopatra liked her cousins, the crowded conditions impressed upon her the importance of having her own space. Most significantly, several years later her immediate family began to break up.

"Where we lived before, having my great-grandmother and grandmother involved in our daily lives was very important. Both of these women helped to keep our family together. They could exercise authority over us and my parents. That kept our family intact. They were role models because they were strong willed, spiritual, and nurturing women."

After they moved, Cleopatra's family no longer had that extended family influence and sense of security that had kept them together.

The family dynamics changed and this has had a major impact upon Cleopatra.

"There was a gradual disintegration of our family after we moved. My parents separated. That to me was a major event. That probably was the most devastating event in my entire life because I didn't realize there were any problems, and then there was this, you know, divorce. I suffered embarrassment. I didn't know what to tell other kids because that kind of thing just didn't happen. That shaped a lot about what I thought about myself as a female and about my need to achieve. Our whole lifestyle changed too after that because my mother then went to work. She had never worked before. She now had to raise four children on her own. She used whatever skills she had learned as a housewife and applied them to the world of work. There were times that she stood in soup lines and had to go on welfare, but she always encouraged me to do my best, even in the toughest of times. She was a model of strength and determination. That was quite an adjustment for her and for all of us. My oldest brother had a major adjustment because he then became the 'man of the house,' in a way, after my Dad was out, and that was hard on him. He was working and bringing money into the house and was still in school.

"There was a lot of stress after we moved. And things were beginning to change. And so I would say that probably, in terms of shaping who I am, that might be one of the single most important events in my life. Change in the structure of the family, from the closeness to ... what I would call the disintegration, change in the way we used to be. We still had family. My mother was still there, but it changed the whole nature of what I was used to.

"Being on welfare for a time was a whole different economic situation. And going into junior high and high school, where there is competition with girls whose fathers are dentists and girls who have nice things, and I worried about whether the soles of my shoes were going to stay on. That has an impact. It caused me to develop an inferiority complex. That was a key point because, while I did well in school—high achiever—on the other hand, I didn't feel good about myself because there were no longer two parents in the house. I felt that it was absolutely devastating not to have both parents in the home. My self-esteem became a bit ruffled. Furthermore, I began to question whether anyone can depend upon a male. So it changed my feelings about dependency upon males, or anyone for that matter, because I was disappointed in many ways. So two things happened. One, I felt the need to make a decision that I didn't want to live this way, that I didn't want to depend upon anybody. I would have my own life. And secondly, I wanted to achieve more than ever. To live independently, I knew I had to achieve."

Cleopatra enjoyed the school environment anyway and spoke positively of her school experiences. "I immediately fell in love with school, probably from day one." Due to several moves, Cleopatra attended a number of schools and enjoyed all of them. "I loved school wherever I went. I loved learning and getting recognized by my teachers, family, and peers for my achievements. That helped my self-esteem, which had been smashed by the disintegration of my family."

As doors opened, Cleopatra took advantage of the opportunities to further her education. Much of her movement up the educational ladder is due to her love of learning, the positive experiences in her school environment, and her firm drive and determination to do well. No one in her family had ever gone to college or knew anything about it. She initially saw it as something unattainable, yet her need for achievement turned into a desire to continue her education. Once she decided that she was going to college, she was committed to the endeavor. Without mentors or other means of support, Cleopatra had to be resourceful in finding a way to make college happen for her. One day during her senior year in high school, Cleopatra decided to talk with a very friendly African American female counselor about her desire to attend college even though she knew that her family could not afford to send her. The counselor then had a conversation with Cleopatra's mother, who did not fully realize the burning desire her daughter had to attend college. Soon thereafter, the counselor helped Cleopatra to obtain a scholarship that opened the door to higher education. Cleopatra's mother, once she understood her daughter's desire, was very supportive. Cleopatra was excited and thrilled that her dream was in the making. Knowing that she would still need more resources, she found a job that provided the supplemental income she needed. For a time she worked several jobs, but she was happy because she had a plan that would ultimately lead to a rewarding life. She had found her ticket to the train bound for success.

Cleopatra states that her chosen focus in college was influenced greatly by her French teacher who was a role model and inspired her to study foreign languages. Cleopatra obtained her bachelors degree in education with a focus in foreign languages (French and Spanish). Her goal was to teach foreign languages in secondary schools. She eventually obtained her masters degree in the area of foreign languages. Due to few jobs teaching foreign languages in the secondary schools at the time she graduated, Cleopatra applied for and obtained a job teaching Spanish at the college level. This sparked her desire to continue at the college level and to seek her doctorate.

With the continued unfavorable job situation in the area of teaching languages, Cleopatra explored other majors. She decided to pursue counseling, another area of great interest to her. She later moved into administration, a shift which she believes to have been influenced by a number of people and experiences in her life. She explains that she accepted a position in a university pre-college program for high school students. The position provided an opportunity to advise and counsel participants. It turned out, however, that the majority of her work was administrative, and she discovered that she enjoys it considerably. She also discovered that she is very talented at it. After talking with several senior administrators and friends, she was encouraged to enroll in a doctoral program in higher education administration. Cleopatra came to believe that administration would allow her to enjoy the best of many worlds. As an administrator she could use her organizational skills, counseling background, and teaching experience to help students to learn and grow. She also noted that as an administrator she would be in a leadership position making decisions that could have positive implications for others. She agreed with the advice of her mentors and friends and enrolled in the higher administration program. She therefore began her lifelong career as an administrator in academia.

Nandi

Nandi's parents also divorced when she was young (six years old). Although she has few memories of her father, she has many rich childhood memories. Nandi grew up in an all-Black neighborhood in East St. Louis, Illinois and is the eighth child of a family of twelve siblings. Nine of the children are girls and three are boys.

"We were impoverished economically but so rich in other ways. I had a strong mother, and she was determined to keep us together after she and my father divorced. There were many people who wanted to adopt us out, but she refused. We lived in the inner city in East St. Louis, Illinois. I had a happy childhood and a loving mother. I was quite talented as a child. I was musically inclined. It just seemed to come naturally. My mother wanted to give me music lessons but she couldn't afford it. But somehow she managed to buy me a piano and I immediately started playing. I could play by ear. But, you know, twelve children playing on a piano ... One day I came home from school and my mother had pushed it out the door and down the steps and had it chopped up. (Laughing.) I wasn't bothered by it. I guess it was just too much for her. I used to paint too. I was on stage all the time. I also did ballet. I never had formal lessons, but the lady down the street made me a tutu, so I was always on the stage. I liked baton, but because my mom could not afford for me to take lessons, my second oldest sister cut an old broomstick down to a baton size and I learned to twirl with that."

Nandi was able to use her talents to open up a way to college. "I became so good [at baton] I even won a scholarship to college competing in baton competitions. That's how I got to college. I went to the University of Illinois to compete, where I won first place. My band director at my high school was so tickled about that. I then was offered a four year scholarship to go to Central State. I kept the scholarship for one year and then decided to teach baton. While I was at Central State I was always singing, dancing, and twirling. I'd teach to offset the college expenses. I even did hair to earn money. I became Miss Central State while I was there. So that's the way my life was. Pretty easy, using whatever natural talents I had so they could really work for me."

Nandi reflects on gifts that she received from her mother that contributed to her own beliefs. "If I could say something I really learned from my mother—she didn't have much, but she was a strong woman. And that reminds me of the old saying: You make a way out of no way. I saw her do that so very often. For instance people thought we were well to do because of our clothes, but we weren't.... I'm not just saying that, but it had to do with the way she kept us. My mother had this old trunk and in that old trunk were dresses and socks and ribbons to match. If you got dressed in the morning and she didn't like the way you looked, she'd go into that old trunk and pull out a ribbon to match what you had on that would just spiff up the outfit, and everyone thought we looked so nice. Everybody remarked about how she kept us.

"My mother, the neighbors, friends, relatives, and teachers were always so nurturing and caring. They really cared about us. I really felt loved during my childhood. Those were the kind of experiences I remember. She never allowed us to go to the corner store without our hair combed, dressed appropriately. You had to have it all together, had to act like a lady. My brothers, not one of them went to prison. Out of twelve children, I think that says a lot for her. Ten of them have degrees from universities, eleven graduated from high school. My mother was elected Mother of the Year by the newspaper. She was always my model. She taught us so much. I still use today what I've learned from her. Several of us have a Masters degree and I of course have my doctorate. So I think that's a credit to her. So it was a good childhood."

Nandi states that the only negative childhood experience she can remember is not having a father to represent her at various functions. Often her brothers and uncles assumed this role. Her father's brothers helped out financially as best as they could. Nandi feels that not having her father there was hurtful at times. Nevertheless, she was surrounded by many caring and nurturing people in her childhood and throughout her school years. She did well in school and describes herself as a very good and conscientious student.

"My teachers cared about me. When I was twirling the [broomstick] baton ... my teachers were fascinated. One made me a majorette outfit. I was always involved in a lot of activities. I've been out front and in leadership positions. Even what I do now is entertaining in some ways and like being on the stage."

Nandi lived in an environment that promoted and encouraged academics. To continue her education after high school was just naturally expected. There have been a number of people in her life that influenced her to take the career path that she has.

"I had a great aunt who was an educator all her life. She certainly was a role model for me. She had a great influence, like a mother figure. And of course my older sisters....when the first two went to college they would come home and debate all the issues of the day, the classics. We younger ones would listen to them, and we wanted to be a part of this. It sounded so great to hear them talk. We wanted to know more about this. We always assumed we'd go to college. We never saw high school as terminal. We had this kind of thing that we'd help each other. The older brother or sister would help the next one, and so on. My mother's pride and her high value of education really influenced me. She was proud of us and she always held herself in high regard. She didn't feel less ... because she didn't have money and never caused us to feel any less because of that. We always had these stimulating debates, heated debates. We didn't know then, but as I look back they were so meaningful and significant. And I think about the language development and how important that was. The older sisters used words we never even heard of, and we'd look them up and start using them just like them. I always assumed I would go beyond the bachelors—not necessarily get a Ph.D.—but the message was to continue on as far as you can go.

"My elementary, junior high, high school, and college were 100% Black. I had such positive role models. We all had so much pride in our teachers and leaders. The teachers, if they saw you walking across campus and your hair was not combed ... would say, 'Go comb your hair.' They cared about every aspect of us. These were the kinds of teachers I had. My first teaching job, in Cleveland, I stayed with my instructor's mother. Here I am, a little kid, didn't know anything. I didn't have a place to stay, so she saw to it that I had a place to stay. Those were the loving caring relationships that were formed. Her mother showed me around. I thank her today for that. That was love—genuine love, unconditional love. My teachers made me feel special. They said 'You want to do that, you can. Nobody ever said you couldn't.' I thought these teachers just had it all together. They took special time and energy. They made students believe they could do anything they wanted to do. I never felt diminished. I had a lot of self-confidence. I felt confident."

Nandi uses the lessons learned as she was growing up in her own teaching. "My first job as a teacher was very enriching. I learned a lot. I learned to demonstrate to the students I was teaching the same love, respect, and encouragement I had been given all my life. I wanted my students to believe they could do anything they set their minds to do. There was this one little African American boy who the principal seemed to dislike. This young man was always in trouble. One day the principal told him that he was going to end up in prison. That infuriated me. I challenged the principal and told him, 'If that is all this young man hears, he will most likely fulfill that expectation, so you, particularly as the principal, have to believe differently about him. Believe in him and hold high expectations for him.' Well that turned the principal around, and the little boy too. Today he is a successful businessman out west."

These early experiences of Nandi have supported her move into leadership positions and academia. "My first marriage didn't work out well. As I reflect back I think not having a dad around during my childhood resulted in me knowing that I have to rely on myself and not be dependent on a man. I think my husband had a hard time with that. Not so much that I was independent in my thinking, but because I was so career and achievement focused. When I went back to school, he couldn't deal with it. Anyway, my second husband has been truly dear to me. He was very supportive as I finished up my doctorate. He supports me totally in my career endeavors now. I've had so many people around me all my life who have encouraged me to 'fly with the eagles.' When I had an opportunity to acquire a position at a university, so many people encouraged me to go for it. Even my children were excited about it."

Nzingha

Nzingha remembers her childhood in a rural area of New York State as a wonderful, nurturing, and enriching experience with many friends and relatives. These early experiences are what enable her to be self-confident.

"Mom and dad lived on a farm. We grew all kinds of food—mostly corn—and we had a small orchard of apples. Those apples were so good. Every fall we would have these social gatherings where relatives and neighbors would come from all around, and we would make cider, wine, and apple jelly. Then sometimes we would go to someone else's house and do the same thing. Everybody chipped in and helped. I loved those times. As it got dark, dad and some of the other men would build a big bond fire, and then, as the fire settled down some, we'd all gather around and roast hot dogs. My favorite part was making s'mores. We had several horses, but my horse, Ginger, loved marshmallows. She used to always try to get into the marshmallows that were for the s'mores. If I wasn't watching, she would grab one.... or two. I guess she liked the sugar in them.

"I had to walk quite a ways to school, but we usually had a lot of fun on the way. Some of my girlfriends and I had this club; we called it the Pony Express. We would all go to our stations in the morning, and since I lived the farthest from the school, I would write out some message and run as fast as I could on my leg of the Pony Express. When I got near Marsha's house, up by her favorite acorn tree, she would be waiting to take the note and run it to the next station. We did this all the way to school. By the time I would arrive at school, the last girl had completed her run and the note would be there waiting on all of us to read and respond to whatever question or issue or riddle would be in it. Sometimes the question was something that had to do with a subject in school. We would make up our own questions, riddles, or math problems. We would try to make them as difficult as we could. A lot of times the questions were about controversial issues that we would debate and argue about. I always had good arguments about whatever the issue was. I remember giving a good argument for not raising the speed limit on the highway and for permitting women to fight in the armed services. I think that experience helped me to be a good lawyer. Our Pony Express club was so much fun.

"I always had chores to do late in the evening, like feeding some of the animals or planting or picking vegetables or fruit and, of course, cleaning up my bedroom. I never had a lot to do around the house during the week because mom and dad wanted me to attend to my school work. They never had to make me do my homework. I always enjoyed doing it.

"I think the most fun part of my childhood was just being around family, friends, our social gatherings; being in school; winning math, writing, and spelling contests; having responsibility around the farm. It made me feel really important. And lastly, I loved being around all my special animals: my horse Ginger, my dog Taylor, and a very special goat I had named Buck. These were my special friends who I could play with, share my food with, and even have them carry my books to school.

"The most difficult part of my childhood was when my brother was killed in a train accident. I was twelve years old. My brother was sixteen and had just learned to drive. He was coming home one evening and stopped by Mrs. Stewart's house. Her dog got loose and he put the dog in the truck and took it up to her. You have to cross a railroad track to get to her house. After returning the dog, he was on his way back home. He must not have seen or heard the train coming. That train smacked into the truck and carried him on down the track. I don't think he ever knew what hit him. When we got the news our whole family was devastated. My brother was wonderful. We did practically everything together. He showed me how to take care of the animals, how to fish and hunt, how to build a fire, how to track wild animals; all kinds of things. I sort of went into seclusion for a while, and it took a long time to for me to come out of that. I read a lot. I think I read to escape to faraway places. But through that experience I became very sensitive to loss and the pain it entails. I learned that life is so tenuous and to appreciate every moment of it. I learned that regardless of the depth of pain one experiences, a person can persevere. I think it helped me to be sensitive to others' pain and to provide whatever support I can, even though I know they must go through the emotion of it on their own.

"My brother's death changed the family a lot, too. Although we continued to have family get-togethers, the former joy we used to have was never there. We had fun, but it seemed like a cloud was always hanging over us. It has taken a long time for that cloud to move on, and even now it seems to reappear every now and then."

Nzingha recalls an educational experience that has had a profound impact on her. "When I was 13 years old and still in my period of seclusion after my brother's death, mom and dad let me go live with one of my aunts and uncles for awhile. I guess they thought getting away from all the things that would bring up memories of my brother would be good. The school I went to had all kinds of clubs. At first I wasn't interested in any of them. There was a debate team and my aunt took me to listen to one of their performances. The debate was on the pros and cons of railroad signs at railroad crossings. The debate truly peaked my interest. Suddenly I saw how the art of communication, things like persuasion, facts, evidence, could be used to drive a point and solicit support from the people. I saw power in that. I went to the next debate where the pros and cons of legalizing marihuana were discussed. It was another year before I actually joined but I did, and it was a great experience for me."

Nzingha states that her desire to go into law was influenced by the debate team, by several relatives who were lawyers, and by TV programs such as Perry Mason. Her desire to help others, especially those who tend to get hurt the most, also influenced her decision.

"I went several times to watch my uncle in court. I was fascinated by what he was able to do. I was really impressed by the way he helped people. Sometimes people, especially African Americans, really get done in by the system. So many things are unfair and it makes me mad. I have another uncle who is a lawyer, too. He has helped some of our people get out of situations that were unfair in the first place. I like that. So I wanted to be able to help in that way.

"I always knew that I would go to college. It was expected. Dad always said, 'If you catch a good one (man), fine, but don't rely on 'em. You've got to be able to do for yourself.' Then I would always say to dad, 'Well you're good to mom and she relies on you.' And he would always respond saying, 'Well, I'm just extraordinary.' That was good advice from dad because there are some trifling guys out there, but there are some extraordinary ones too. Although I'm currently single, I am now engaged to an extraordinary one.

"After high school, I went to college and then continued on into Law School. I graduated with honors and began practicing law with a firm near the university. I was there for about a year and then moved here to practice law. After being here for a few years, I was encouraged by many colleagues to take a position at the university that was open. I did and so here I am, teaching others something I truly enjoy."

Tiye

Tiye grew up in a predominantly African American urban neighborhood in a large midwestern city. Many of her relatives lived within walking distance of her parent's home.

"I felt like I had moms and dads all over the place. My second cousin and his wife lived two streets to the north of us; one aunt and uncle lived one street south of us; another aunt and uncle lived four streets to the south of us; and another aunt and uncle lived one street to the north of us. They were all within walking distance. And then I had a host of other relatives throughout the city. The neighbors on the street all knew us and we knew them. My mom and dad would visit them and they would visit us. The kids all played together. We had our little arguments and fights with some of the neighbor kids, but for the most part we got along and played together. You don't see much of that today. Dinner time was special because we would all sit together and eat and discuss all kinds of ideas and issues. You don't see much of that either.

"We also had a lot of professionals and prominent people who lived on our street—doctors, dentists, teachers, preachers, well-known sports figures who played with the professional teams. As a child, I was able to go to many games free because my father and the sportsmen were friends. I can remember even going up in the press box. We really had a lot of well-educated and well-known Black folks on our street, and they were all down-to-earth people. I loved it. I have many fond memories of that neighborhood. My parents lived there for fifty years. We (my brother, sister, and I) and my cousins and other relatives always gathered there at the house and had big holiday celebrations and dinners all the time."

Tiye remembers her childhood as one of much security, love, and nurturance. She had a lot of exposure to prominent African Americans who had excelled, reached many of their dreams, and were very successful in their careers. Her parents were also successful in their careers and highly respected throughout the community. "With so many career oriented and successful people around me, it just seemed natural that I would follow a similar path. I had wonderful role models all around me."

Tiye is very talented and her secure upbringing allowed her the opportunity to develop many of her talents. These early years of Tiye were filled with dance lessons, piano lessons, travel clubs, and a variety of youth groups. These opportunities have helped to shape who Tiye is today.

Her early experiences were also filled with many church and spiritual experiences. "My grandmothers and mother were church goers and believed that faith in God was everything. Whenever things got rough, they prayed. I saw their reliance upon faith in God to get them through difficult situations as very powerful. Dad didn't go to church much, but mom made sure we attended Sunday school regularly. I enjoyed being in the plays and presentations at church. I was always afraid to get up in front of other people, but I love performing.

"I felt especially sensitive to the struggles and hurts of others, whether people, animals, or plants. I remember one time some neighbor boys grabbed a cat, put a rope around its neck, and hung it in a tree. I immediately ran to hold the cat up and demanded that these older boys untie the rope from the cat's neck. I was enraged by their mistreatment of a helpless animal.

"I feel like my childhood was very rich. My parents never really had a lot of opportunities, so they wanted to make sure my brother, sister, and I were able to do all the things they didn't have a chance to do. So, I took piano lessons and dance lessons. I loved them both, and at one time I thought I would become a great composer of music. Then I thought I would become a famous dancer. I took ballet, tap, jazz, interpretive. I even went to a university near my home and took Spanish lessons in the summer. I never took art lessons, but I love to draw and paint and I've always been pretty good at it. I joined a travel club, too, and we held all kinds of fund raisers and traveled many places. I belonged to a lot of other clubs, too, so I was very active and involved in things.

"As a child, I played a lot in the neighborhood. I must have been very athletic and competitive because, when I think back, I was the fastest runner and the fastest bicyclist on my street. I could climb trees and rugged hills faster and better than anyone around. I loved to read, too. I liked being alone to read and to watch and study nature. I used to love to watch the birds. I had a garden and I really cared for each and every plant and would sometimes cry when one would get hurt. Although I thinned the vegetables, I really didn't like to because I felt that each little plant should have an opportunity to survive. I guess I just wanted everything to grow to its fullest.

"That's probably why I went into the field of teaching and counseling. There are so many things that happen to people that keep them from living to their fullest. I think that as a teacher and counselor I can help people change unfulfilling situations in their lives so that they can live life more fully."

From the time Tiye was a very young child, she has always known that she would go to college. By the age of ten, she had already decided she would study psychology and continue in school as far as she could. "College was never a question. Mom and other family members had gone to college. It was just an assumed expectation because when we talked about education, my parents spoke in terms of 'when' you go, not 'if' you go."

Tiye states that her chosen area of study was influenced mostly by relatives who were teachers, relatives who were always helping others, movies like the *Three Faces of Eve*, her desire to help others, and her fascination with others' behaviors and trying to understand the way they function. "I remember watching the movie *Three Faces of Eve* and thinking I would like to be a person who sits in an office and listens to others' problems and try to help them. I think I was about eleven or twelve years old then. I was always helping others and finding ways to do something nice for someone. Many of the kids on the street would talk with me about all kinds of things. I guess they came to me because I was a good listener. I didn't like to talk much myself, but I would certainly listen.

"My most difficult educational experience was when I went to college and one of my White roommates did not like me simply because I was Black. She didn't want to touch me nor want me to touch her or her belongings. She acted like I was dirty. When we were with other people, she would try to act friendly in front of my face and then talk about me like a dog when I wasn't there. It was difficult living with someone whom I knew despised me. And she disliked me for something I could not change. It didn't make sense. At times I felt really uncomfortable, but when she asked me to move out, I stood my ground and told her that if she was having a problem, then she needed to move out. At the end of the first semester, she did just that. That was the first time I had experienced someone who was really blatantly racist, and initially it left me frustrated and confused. But I think with so many supportive people in my life, I was able to still feel good about myself and see it as her problem.

"Years later, I had several experiences with racist attitudes when I was unable to find housing. Everywhere I went, I was turned down, and the owners would have some excuse for not renting the apartment or house to me. Sometimes the owners would ask me to come and see the apartment or house and then when I would arrive, they would say that they just rented the place to a relative or that a storm caused some damage and the place could not be rented now. Lies, lies, lies. They didn't want to rent because of the color of my skin. Those encounters left me really angry and bitter toward biased people. It's interesting that I never generalized that feeling to all White people, but the notion of discrimination, racism, oppression, maltreatment just infuriates me.

"Another difficult educational experience was several years later when I wanted to enter graduate school. I didn't do well on one of the standardized tests for entrance. When I was told I had scored below the cut off and would not be accepted, my initial reaction was one of extreme hurt and disappointment. Even then, I thought I would just take the test again. But, when the lady who was collecting the tests told me that I was not graduate material, I felt crushed by a power and a system that had no idea who I was and cared less about my hopes and dreams. My heart sank all the way to the floor—below the floor. I was devastated. I questioned my abilities for a brief moment. But what I noticed was that that question did not stay with me long, and I became angry with the testing policy. I had to challenge it. I began figuring a way in which I would be able to attend graduate school anyway. Regardless of the test results, I knew that I was just as capable as anyone else. Within a week, I wrote a letter to the university challenging the purpose and reliability of the test, speaking of past accomplishments, and assuring them that I had every belief in my ability to do well in graduate school. About two weeks later I received an acceptance letter from the university. After the first year of classes I had straight A's, and some of those in my class who had done well on the entrance exams had grade point averages of 1.0 or less. My family background gave me that belief and courage to take on challenges like that. So when I started my Ph.D., I knew I would succeed in getting it. That, in turn, opened the door for me to take on a tenure tracked position at the university level. The thrill and excitement of a new challenge led me to this position."

Amina

Amina has also had wonderful childhood experiences. Her most memorable childhood experiences center around living in an extended family and experiencing being the fifth living generation.

"Ah, when I was born I was the fifth living generation in my family at that time. I knew my great grandparents and my great-great-grandparents on my mother's side of the family. I knew a lot about their backgrounds. I knew a lot about my great-great-grandfather's years in slavery. I knew about him. He had his freedom papers. It was the first time I had ever heard of this oxymoron called a free slave.

"I knew my Native American relatives as well. And that's an area that I don't really delve into very much and I should do more, but my great-great-grandfather was pure African and very proud of it. And I took his picture with me one time to West Africa, and so they told me where he was from. I haven't gone there yet to dig up his roots, but they looked at his face and they said, 'We know where this guy's from.'"

Amina was born and raised in New York and lived in a Black community where people from many areas—the Caribbean, Africa, Puerto Rico—lived together. She states that with this exposure she grew up speaking Spanish and English, and her exposure to many prominent personalities was just a natural part of her upbringing.

"My mother's mother danced with Josephine Baker in Cotton Club. She was a singer and involved in theater. My grandfather was Gula, so he and my uncle and his brother spoke Geeche, and I would try to learn it too. But my grandfather wouldn't allow me to speak it because he said it would prevent me from mainstreaming. So whenever I was around, he ... and the others would stop speaking because they knew I was picking it up. The man carrying the flag in the picture of the 369 coming back from World War I is my great-grandfather. Sidney Poitier owned the club down the street that my mother worked in for a while. You know, there were people in and out and I just never paid any mind, so I've never been star struck or anything. I mean, they were always just human beings. So it was kind of just a nice sort of eclectic environment. My grandfather was a bootlegger amongst other things, so I had a very colorful childhood to say the least."

Although Amina's family started out in Harlem, they moved to Queens, and that is where she was raised and went to a Catholic school. Her experiences in school were not as pleasant as her childhood home and community environment. She describes many of her school experiences as devastating, although she feels she received a good education.

"We did get a good education, but it was absolute torture. I have asthma, so invariably in the beginning of every fall semester I was not in school.... Because I was sick and sometimes hospitalized, it was troubling and very trying. I could say that for the most part the nuns were very supportive just because I liked to study and that kind of thing. In elementary school it wasn't quite as testy as it got to be when I went to Catholic high school, and eventually I left because of that. But I remember in the first grade somebody dropped a wallet on the floor, and in my stupidity I went and picked it up and took it to the principal's office.... They accused me of taking the wallet and put me in the closet. Two of these nuns were standing over me dressed completely in black and basically torturing me about what I had done with this money and where was the money, and you took it, and you know you took it. And after that I just ... every time I see anything I just leave it. I will not even touch it. That just left such an impression on me.

"Also there was the contradiction between living in an all Black environment and going into this other environment for my education. My great-grandmother was very good at preparing me for that. She said 'Go in there and get everything you got and don't come home with none of those folks' bad habits,' and I'm cleaning ... up the way she said it.... I have lived by that all of my life.

"Now high school was torture because Forest Hills High School was originally all White. After desegregation the Black kids went to Forest Hills, and we fought everyday. Every single solitary day there was a fight. And either somebody was pushing somebody down the stairs, or up the stairs, or tripping them, or something. It was absolutely amazing. It did settle down a bit, but not much. It was torment.

"One year when I was really sick with asthma almost the whole academic year ... my friends would bring my homework to me. So I did my homework and I would send it back, and consistently I was at the top of the class in math and English. I love math and I love English. Anyway, the two worst educational experiences that I had were, first, when I got to the eighth grade and graduated with honors and awards and stuff. Well, the person who was closest to me was a White girl. She didn't have asthma. So what they decided to do, when I came back after being sick for three weeks, is to give us a test. They tested Agnes and me. I still didn't feel too well. They decided that Agnes beat me by two points and that Agnes would get the school award, first place in math. I was devastated. I was absolutely devastated because this had been my award first from the first to the eighth grade, and I had been at the top of the line all the way through. Well, the day of graduation they called Agnes' name ... as the first place, and they called me as second place. I refused to stand up. The nuns came over to me and said, 'You have to stand up.' I said, 'I don't have to do anything. I'm finished with you.' And I refused to stand up in the church where the ceremony was held. My mother was very upset. And I told her, I said, 'I'm not a second place person, and I'm not standing up second place to anybody.'

"That experience set me off on the wrong foot when I went to high school. I never recovered. It was war in high school. But I've always loved to learn and I loved math. I was supposed to be a mathematician.

"The second experience was when I was advancing so well in math, algebra, and all.... Well, I finished the math book for the ninth grade before everybody else. I wanted more math, but the teachers refused to give me more. They even locked me out of the library. When my class went to the library I had to sit outside the library. Instead of putting me in an advanced class, they told me I had gone too far ahead of everybody and that I was really a problem and that the best thing for me to do was to sit over here and just shut up and be quiet. I really began to hate them. And the day when it finally just all flew apart was one day with ... this one nun, my French teacher. Well I'd get in class and I knew all the stuff, so she would just look right over top of me and ignore me. And I had my hair in a French twist. But she kept ignoring me.... After class I must have really gotten loud, so she went and she pulled my hair ... out of the twist.... She told me: 'Niggers don't wear French twists. Niggers wear braids. And niggers don't speak French either.' I turned around and walloped her. I'm not very good at this patience stuff. Well they told my mother and she was upset. I told her I just could not take anymore.

"I went back to school for a while, and it just got increasingly worse. I mean, you know, they ... it was always something, and they just called me nigger one too many times, and that was it. I told my mother, I said either you take me out or I'm dropping out. So eventually my mother took me out. That's when I went to Forest Hills, but that did not solve my problems. My government teacher said he did not believe that I was an American Negro because I knew too much and I came from a Catholic background. 'You know, you're getting a good education.... You couldn't possibly be an American Negro.... What country did you grow up in?' When I told him I lived down the street, he had me taken out of his class and put back in American History I."

Amina feels that much of her educational career path has been influenced by the tremendous exposure she had to so many different people from around the world and just by being in New York City.

"The U.N. was one of my favorite places. I grew up near LaGuardia Airport, so I would walk down and watch the planes coming and see all these people getting off the planes and speaking different languages and all that kind of stuff. It really piqued my curiosity. I didn't want to grow up in the same neighborhood and die in the same place. I didn't want that life. Education I did see as an out."

Although Amina wanted to be a mathematician, the racism she encountered forced her out of that choice. A French teacher who took a liking to her got her back into humanities, in which she enjoyed mythology, literature, and writing. She then moved to Black Studies because she could see its relevancy and knew from her own experience that African Americans should be getting more out of life. During her college years, Amina was exposed to many brilliant and prominent people. One of the things that is now difficult for Amina as a full professor is knowing that as a people we can do better. Amina is frustrated with how we, as African Americans, short change ourselves.

Summary

If we had been gazing into a crystal ball, we might have easily predicted that these women were destined for success. What are the elements of their childhood that make this so? All of the study participants grew up in predominantly African American or ethnically mixed neighborhoods and had many family members and neighbors around who were very supportive. They began their lives knowing that they came into and belonged to communities of people who valued them greatly. They had many parents throughout their neighborhoods to teach and to raise them. Their family and role models instilled in these women the belief that they were loved, as well as the notion that they could fulfill any dream they held. They saw that their worth was a given, without question.

All of the women were not only encouraged but were expected to express themselves and to utilize their talents in many ways. They were given the time and space necessary to explore and develop their talents. Somé (1998) stated that people crave two things: (1) the full realization of their innate gifts and (2) the acknowledgement, approval, and confirmation of their gifts through community. These women were supported in the development and implementation of their gifts, regardless of the resources or lack of resources their families had. Also, their inquisitive nature was fed through the various activities they participated in. The support and encouragement they had to reach for the heavens, coupled with their intellectual capacity, imparted in these women the belief that they could do anything they chose to do.

Our study participants were exposed to many positive role models, even some who were quite famous. They witnessed first hand the numerous possibilities and opportunities for African Americans and the important values necessary for positive living. Thus they were instilled with the notion of entitlement to such possibilities.

They have also witnessed either their parents or grandparents utilizing faith and the power of prayer to deal with difficult situations, instilling in these women the importance of faith and spirituality in their lives as a means of reaching their goals and helping others. Although their goals, at times, seemed impossible, they held to a belief that all things are possible and that there was spiritual power directing and guiding their life journeys. Even with seemingly insurmountable obstacles, each of the women went to college, completed undergraduate and graduate degrees in their respective disciplines, and pursued careers in higher education.

In addition, each of the women encountered experiences that challenged their sense of self. They endured situations that implied that their essence was flawed. Although these experiences would leave them shaken, they recovered quickly. They have been through the kiln only to come out stronger. With the rich affirmations from their families and communities, and in some cases from their churches, they acquired a positive sense of self and a strong internal fighting spirit that challenges negative implications and demonstrates to others that they are as good as anyone else.

While several of the women are married, they were all raised to believe that they did not have to be dependent upon men for their own personal welfare. They were encouraged early to work, to obtain a career, and to support themselves. They were not confined in their thinking to traditional roles of womanhood.

These are clearly women who have developed the characteristics of kujichagulia (self-determination). They have developed the drive, fortitude, intelligence, confidence, and foundational support necessary to survive in a sometimes hostile, racially prejudiced environment. We can see that through their power of self-determination, enhanced by their childhood environments, these African American women have been able to transcend the confines of obstacles and oppression. If we were to make a list of significant characteristics that the study participants possess, the following descriptions would characterize them:

Committed	Inquisitive	Open to the new	Innovative
Healthy	Team player	Active	Self-assured
Visionary	Self-challenging	Persevering	
Assertive	Reflective	Challenging of others	

Expectation of entitlement to the same rights as others

CHAPTER 3
Ujima
The Realities of Academia

Cross the river in a crowd and the crocodile won't eat you.
(African Proverb)

When we have a problem or an issue, we often think that we are either the problem or its cause. We consider the assaults to our personhood as personal troubles rather than as social issues. Friere (1970/2001) stated that individuals unaware of the connections between their own lives and society personalize their problems. Even if we realize that others may have similar concerns, as African American women our isolation in separate departments and program areas throughout the academy often prevents us from mobilizing necessary resources to resolve the problems.

One objective of this chapter is to bring to the forefront the reality of academic life for African American women so that common thoughts and concerns are identified. With awareness and recognition of common concerns, African Americans and other academic personnel can formulate means for addressing such concerns. When individuals work together, much can be accomplished. As the Seneca people say: "He who would do great things should not attempt them all alone." When African American faculty and administrators work together, assuming collective responsibility (ujima) for raising the issues and solving common problems, they form a strong bond of support that is necessary for survival and for creating change in academia. When both African American and non-African American academic personnel assume collective responsibility (ujima), they also form a bond necessary for addressing the issues and creating change. Developing supportive relationships and collective responsibility in the academic setting does not come easily, however, as we shall see in the stories of these women's experiences.

Academia has traditionally been a competitive, individualistic environment where academicians set personal goals and often work alone. Faculty in particular are encouraged to engage in research and to function independently. For example, greater recognition often comes to those who have single authorship in research articles and books than to co-authors. Faculty members are often encouraged to direct their interests to areas where others have not delved. Ideas, writings, research, and teaching are most valuable when they are most distinctive. Competition for funding sometimes works against collaboration within departments. Although beginning and untenured faculty are referred to as junior faculty, they are frequently left to traverse the tenure and promotion track alone with little guidance or mentoring. Administrators serve in departments that are different and have varying issues. They may feel alone and isolated in managing their specific issues. Furthermore, universities have historically been isolated from and unrelated to the communities in which they exist. These traditional practices in the university counter the value system of many African Americans, particularly women—a value system which fosters community, connection, and relevancy to the area in which they work.

Let us now hear from the women themselves. This chapter captures the common themes in the women's perspectives about their fulfilling experiences as well as the obstacles and struggles they encounter in academia. We obtain a view of the survival strategies and support systems that sustain these women as they attempt to build their careers in predominantly White institutions.

Cleopatra

Cleopatra, the dean of a college at a midwestern university, tells us about her commitment to her work and her students. "What motivates me is that I really like to be around students, and that's the reason I made the ... shift toward student development.... I'll either get involved in some activity where I can work with them, serve on a doctoral committee or a research project, or teach a class. It's a joy to be around students.

"You know, I was thinking of Black students that I met in South Africa who were formerly at all White Universities; how exciting that was to just walk and talk with them.... I really like that kind of interaction. I really do miss it. So I try to do things that will keep me, in some ways, in touch with them.

"It's not just the position I hold. That doesn't really turn me on unless there is something there I can do to benefit primarily my own people; ... my goal is always the liberation of Black people. So, whatever route I have to take to do that, then so be it. So I suspect that wherever I am if there are people of color who are oppressed ... that I would probably be committed to this."

Cleopatra enjoys being with students and sees herself as an advocate for students' needs as well as for their educational and career advancement. The desire to have a positive impact on the lives of others, particularly African American students, has been an important theme throughout the life of Cleopatra. Taking action on behalf of the students is truly a motivating factor. She excitedly tells us: "What else motivates me? I would say, helping people. I consider myself a helping professional. That motivates me. If I can in some way help to improve the quality of somebody's life, or make a difference, or help them make a choice that will improve their life or their situation, that's what motivates me."

After having her own self-esteem shaken during the time of her parents' separation, Cleopatra began reading a lot of psychology books and thought, even at that time, of going into counseling. Her career path, however, ultimately led to administration where she has been able to fulfill counseling, mentorship, and advocacy roles.

Fulfilling these roles keeps Cleopatra excited about her work and brings her a great deal of satisfaction.

As a college dean, Cleopatra is involved in planning, seeking funds, managing personnel, and developing programs based on future outlook. She speaks with confidence of her skill in these areas, but she also speaks of her need to move on to other interests and concerns. "I consider myself a builder of programs, and I guess I've done that most of my career. I usually start with a core of programs and add others.... And then you get to a point in the organization where you kind of recognize that there is only so far you can go with that.... I tend to think that new leadership is good after a certain period. You get new ideas. I wear out with a thing after a while, so I have to reach out to other challenges."

Cleopatra tells an interesting story about the challenges, rewards, and frustrations she has encountered along her career path at two distinctly different institutions: "Early in my administrative career, I was fortunate to be in a very hospitable and nurturing environment. I spent several good years at an urban community college where there were many African Americans (men and women) in key positions. The president was African American, as well as many vice presidents and deans. I considered a number of these people to be role models and mentors. I felt that my competence and my potential were recognized, valued, and rewarded. I was promoted quite a few times after I demonstrated that I was capable of assuming greater responsibility. I was ultimately promoted to the position of dean, and I believe I could have gone further had I remained at the institution. While this environment was in no way problem-free, I rarely felt that my race or gender was an issue. In fact, this was a place where diversity of race, gender, and ethnicity was very evident in all categories: administrative, faculty, and students. I was also generally well respected by my colleagues, staff, and [the] students that I served. As I look back on this period of time, I think these were probably the best years of my professional career."

Cleopatra tells quite a different story about her experience at a predominantly White institution; it is indeed a "picture of a different color." "I was the first African American and the first female dean of my college. And I am still, after many years, the only black female dean in the institution. Although I competed 'fair and square' for this position through a national search, there were early and immediate challenges to my status and leadership. These 'boos and hisses' came primarily from some White females in subordinate positions who, in my view, had difficulty with a Black woman in a position of considerable authority. I brought a totally new and different cultural worldview and leadership style. For a variety of reasons, they did not support me. Some left subsequently, and it was probably for the best. Many challenges remained, however.

"In all fairness, I have had considerable support from my dean colleagues and other key individuals. They have helped to make the experience overall a positive one. Having said that, there are still times when I have felt like I don't belong here; I have felt like I was in the wrong place and wanted to go back to where I belong, where I had a better fit, and frankly where I could do more good.

"What troubles me most is what I call the 'seamier side,' the underbelly of the institution—that is, institutional racism. Institutional racism is real, pervasive, and intense. I've witnessed it occur with Black students, faculty, and support staff. I see its harsh effect upon programs and services that are designed to assist Black students. These programs seem to be of low priority, undervalued, under funded, and marginalized. While there is an espoused commitment to diversity and inclusion, the reality defies the rhetoric. There are still too few African Americans and other people of color in this institution.... I know this is the case in most White institutions, but I still don't like it. And I mean no disrespect to those Whites and people of color who continue to work hard to change the complexion and the climate of the institution.

"I think I was somewhat naive about the race issue before I assumed the role of dean at this PWI. I think it was because of the kind of environment that I had become accustomed to at an urban community college, where I honed my administrative skills. I was protected from blatant examples of racism and sexism.... It really wasn't until I had my own personal encounter with these twin evils in my current role that I realized how devastating the experience can be. What is more painful is that some of our own people work against us; they literally help the White establishment perpetuate discriminatory practices. I think that some Black folk lose their minds, souls, and identities when they come to these White campuses. Some of them won't associate with anything Black on campus. They fail to realize that no one respects a person who is a traitor to his own people. What good is all of this education if we don't use it to uplift our race? When we lift ourselves, we lift everybody. I am so tired of Black folk fighting each other. We don't have the luxury of engaging in 'petty Black politics' when there's a war going on. How can we fight racism, and ensure our own survival, when we're pointing guns at each other?"

To Cleopatra success is being able to make good on your dreams and being happy with your choices. "I dreamed about education and being in education, and I have been fortunate to be able to fall into many areas of higher education, all of which I really enjoy.... To me that is success: having been able to do that and also having been able to do that at higher levels each time. It's like a spiral just going up. So I think that, to me, success is being able to make the choices you want to make, being in the environment you want to be in, being in the profession you have chosen for life and really liking it. I think it would be devastating to be in a field you didn't like.

"I loved school, so it was natural for me to keep going until I obtained my Ph.D. I feel very proud of that accomplishment. I am happy that I am working in a profession that I truly love and have a great deal of freedom.

Cleopatra notes that as an administrator she does not have a great deal of time to pursue research and to get papers published. However, she does co-author with colleagues who have similar interests. "Working with someone is more effective for me in meeting my research and publication agenda. With my responsibilities, if it wasn't for collaborating with someone else, I don't think I would be able to research and complete papers for publication."

Nandi

Nandi, the Associate Professor in Business Education at a midwestern university, shares how life changed for her when she moved from her African American community into the mostly

White university system. Nandi's experiences in graduate school and in her professional life are different than those in her childhood because she is now around mostly non-African Americans. In these settings she does not experience the caring, nurturing environment that she previously knew. However, she feels that her background enables her to have the confidence necessary to do well and to handle effectively and without malice or hostility the biases and oppressions she encounters.

"When I came here, I initially had to establish myself ... I had to prove myself. All eyes were on me. I had to be cautious about the way I dressed, my demeanor, and what I said or did, because everyone was watching. The students had a certain mind set and I had to cut through some of that. Now that I've been here a while, this is not a problem. I've developed a reputation as being fair, very professional, and having high expectations of students and colleagues. I don't have to prove myself now, but I didn't have to prove myself in this way in all-Black settings. I was expected to do well, and I was treated as though people knew I would do well.

"As a person of color, I was expected to be a representative on so many committees. I've learned that I have to choose which committees to join ... to develop alternatives, and to keep going. I cannot respond to all the requests. However, some things cannot be ignored. I deal with issues head-on and with respect. For my own self preservation, I have to choose. I don't have people stand up for me, either, for things I can do myself. I don't want to be seen as weak, and so if I have to challenge someone, then I do it. There is racism in the institution, for example, regarding research on African Americans. Many Whites don't understand that research, and so they do not value it as highly. Thus, I had to publish even more so because of the lesser value placed on research about African Americans as I went through the tenure and promotion process.

"When I think about why I continue to work in academia even with the obstacles, it is because I enjoy helping students and I love the intellectual stimulation. There are always guest speakers, discussions with colleagues and students, and research. There is always the glow of a student who has found new personal growth because of his or her learnings. These things keep me excited about life and about being in academia. I feel stimulated, inspired. I love it!"

Nandi views herself as a successful person in that she has held positions whereby she can provide access for others. "When I am in a position where I can advocate for a student or help a student to reach his or her goals, then I feel successful and powerful in what I am doing. I try to help others in the way that so many people helped me. I remember meeting a student who had applied to the Ph.D. program three times and had not been accepted. She was in my class, and I saw the potential she had. After looking at her paperwork, I noticed she did not present herself well and basically didn't know how to do so. With some feedback on how to more effectively present her application packet, she was on her way. Another time a group of students had been treated with bias by one of the campus organizations. After much discussion and advocating for the students, the restrictions placed on them were lifted."

Nandi knew that, as faculty, she had to engage in research and to submit articles for publication in order to obtain an associate level position and full professorship. This proved difficult for Nandi. "It is a struggle, and I have to carve out hours of the day and night to engage in research and to get articles published. It's not easy. I am excited about my research areas, but finding sufficient time to develop manuscripts is hard. For me writing requires a large bulk of time to really concentrate, reflect, and delve into what I'm writing about. Where do I find this large bulk of time when I'm asked to be involved in so many other things? It's not easy to balance being a team player and trying to do my own research. Early on I found myself getting pulled in numerous directions.... I think what finally has made it work for me is that I had to come to the realization of the importance of publication for my career and my goals and to say 'no' to the many university expectations. After all, it's my career and my life. If I'm going to contribute to my profession and be successful within my profession, I must focus on that and not on the numerous demands of the university, college, and department. To gain even more respect from my students and colleagues, I knew I needed to be seen as a leader in my area of research. Research has become a priority, and thus if I am asked to serve the university or community,

I stop to think how this service will enhance my research agenda. I had to make choices about my career and my contribution to the profession I love. It's a matter of choices. I think sometimes we are afraid to say 'no' or feel guilty doing so, but I've found that I'm even more respected for having done so."

A friend of Nandi's acknowledges that she is very meticulous about, passionate in, and dedicated to her work. "I think what has really helped Nandi succeed is her passion for what she does. She really attracts people to her; they like her, and she is definitely a motivator. She can talk about most anything because she has had so many experiences. On the down side, though, Nandi worries whether she has done enough."

Nzingha

The road to full professorship has been rewarding, yet it has demanded the sacrifice of much of Nzingha's time. "An African American woman in academia, in the Law Department, and a full professor. Wow! I love it! I love what I do! But, it hasn't been easy. First, I've had to sacrifice a lot of time away from my family and friends. Now that I'm older, I wish at times I could have spent more time with them. I've never taken time to really develop a relationship with a guy. I've dated a few, but so much of my time and effort has been in work. The guys I've dated just weren't able to deal with that, and I didn't do much to nourish the relationships either. I'm hoping things will be better with the guy I'm dating now."

The desire to impact positively others' lives has been an important theme in the life of Nzingha. "I think I am motivated by the desire to help others. I like knowing that I can be of assistance to others. What I like about my job is the impact I have on students, being with students, and the contribution I feel I'm making in terms of the research I do in the area of law. I am highly regarded in the profession and deliver quite a few speeches. Because of this high regard, it is difficult for colleagues to discount me, which I know sometimes that is what they want to do because I'm Black and because I'm a woman. Sometimes I might want to do something a little differently than it has been done in the past, but I get questioned. I'm sure if it was a

White male doing the same thing, colleagues would think, 'Wow, how innovative.' But no, they want to question my intentions and purpose.

"Before I became a full professor, it seemed as though I had to always justify why I was doing what I was doing. It wouldn't be so bad if my colleagues were getting the same treatment, but they weren't. I've come to realize that my classes tend to be more interactive and relational. Many students are used to a more traditional way of operating in class, with lectures and being told what to think and do—where the professor is the expert and students are the learners. But I bring a style that functions as a collaborative community of thinkers. While some students love it, some don't seem to be able to handle that. Stereotypes pop up and they view me as lacking in expertise, intellectually inferior, incompetent, and thus initially my teaching evaluations were low. I received a lot of flack from my colleagues because of my low teaching evaluations. This kept me nervous and extremely depressed at times. It even appeared that my contract would not be renewed. But there was no concrete evidence of poor teaching. In fact, my chair observed me only once and gave me very little feedback. I then decided to focus on my research. I think over time they've seen my writings, my books; they've seen me operate in meetings and they know that I have expertise. Word gets around and I do not have to prove myself to students and colleagues now. I suppose all faculty have to go through a stage of proving themselves to some extent, but when race and gender are factors, stereotypes abound and the process is just more complex and challenging.

"My value system seems to always be in conflict with the rest of the university and my colleagues. Where they put emphasis on financial, structural, and organizational matters, I place more emphasis on people concerns. Where I put emphasis on inclusion and encouragement of people and on faith in their potential, they put emphasis on criteria for exclusion of people. When I see African American students treated unfairly, I get mad and I want to fight; I want to do something to help them. I get tired in my attempts to do so, but I get frustrated because sometimes there are so many battles to fight. I can't fight them all. I think sometimes I actually feel bad that I can't be there to help in all situations. Cognitively I know that I cannot fight every battle, but in my heart I still get stressed over the fact that I can't help everyone."

In responding to how she deals with racism and sexism, Nzingha states, "I get angry. I'm really mad sometimes, and I let others know just how I feel. I guess by venting I get rid of some of the frustration, but then they think I'm this crazy Black woman who has just gone off. Sometimes what I say gets discounted as a crazy woman, but I think I do get people to stop and listen and think sometimes. They know I'm right a lot of the times, whether they want to admit it or not. So I get mad and confused. And that's because sometimes I feel so alone, rejected, and I wonder if it is just me. I wonder what is really going on here.

"I think that now I'm a little more attuned to the political or power dynamics that go on, so it's not so confusing now, and I feel stronger in standing my ground. But it wasn't always easy. Sometimes I just quietly figure a way to work around or redirect the situation. A lot of times I use reason and argument (my law background and skills, and my gift of gab) and my persuasive voice to deal with a situation. I can stay calm and my calmness during tense times is just the ingredient to get others to think clearly. But being rational and clear thinking doesn't always work, especially during tense racial situations, and people get all bent out of shape and emotional. Then they can't listen to reason. I usually have to approach them later when they are more sane. I guess I just challenge racism and sexism when I can, but sometimes I just have to throw up my hands and keep on movin' on because I can't deal with it all. Sometimes White folks just don't know, and I have to play this role of educating them. They don't recognize racism. Men often don't recognize sexism. People in power positions don't recognize what they do to the powerless. They have to be taught, but why do I have to educate them all the time? I need my rest, too. Sometimes I have to [chuck] it to the wind because no one can force people to be appreciative and respectful of others' differences. And I pray a lot. I pray that the Lord will help me to do what is necessary and appropriate, I pray for my own peace of mind and health, and I pray that in the long run, perhaps through divine intervention, things are going to work out anyway. I really believe that if we trust in God, that things will work out to benefit the underdog anyway."

Although Nzingha has achieved much during her life, it has only been within recent years that she sees herself as successful. "Success to me is when you do something that really makes a difference in the lives of others and when that something is rather permanent. For example, I have always done a lot of things to help people and to impact ... their lives positively, but if some tragedy or crisis came up, all that I had done previously could easily be undone. I guess when you can impact positively in such a way that it's enduring—no one can come along tomorrow and take it away—like changing a law, or putting in place a program or idea, or changing systemically the organizational structure such that it's going to be there for awhile and many people will benefit from it ... to me that's rewarding; that's success. What good is my success if I'm the only one that benefits? How can I feel successful if all of my people are oppressed? Success is when many can share the benefits. So whatever my position, if I can impact in such a way that ... systemic change occurs that makes a difference, then that is success. Even if it's a book or article that presents ideas and enables people to feel more empowered, then that book or article has left a permanent mark that makes a difference.

"Some would see the acquisition of full professorship as successful. Full professorship allows me the freedom, to some extent, to be left alone to do those things I define as meaningful, and that is making change to benefit many others.

"Reaching full professorship wasn't easy. It took me a while to define an area of research. I needed a mentor, someone to help me be focused on the important things that needed to be accomplished. So it took me a few years to figure the whole research thing out. Once I identified for myself what I wanted to spend my life and career doing, once I identified what my passion for research was, then I took off, delving into whatever I could regarding my research. I talked about my topic with students and colleagues, and I sort of became identified with my area of research. As I did so, colleagues who had similar interests became involved, and we sort of had a group thing going of researching and writing together. Not all of us were at the same university, so that made it interesting."

Tiye

Academia has been rewarding for Tiye, an associate professor in the Counseling Department at a midwestern university, but it has also been difficult. "I love being a college professor. It has been very rewarding assisting students in their own careers. To see them grow and become more than perhaps what they ever thought they would become is so fulfilling to me. Also, I love being a leader in my profession. It's wonderful to deliver workshops and write articles and have people respect you for your ideas and what you do."

However, Tiye notes: "When I first came here, everyone welcomed me, but soon after getting started, I noticed how alone I was. Of course the autonomy was great, but with all the attention received during the recruitment and hiring process, it was such a drastic change after I began working here. I felt abandoned, like I had been dropped off in a world of total isolation. With no mentoring and excluded from the informal network system and conversations, I felt completely in the dark. When I mentioned some of my concerns, others responded by questioning me with, 'What is the problem?' I thought, well maybe this is the way academia is and I just needed to fit in and learn that this is how it is going to be. But I was uncomfortable and began watching and listening to others' experiences. It took a long time to realize that this did not have to be the way academia is and that I can work toward change. The isolation kept me down, but it was through the connections I was making with other African American and European-American women and through hearing their experiences that academia changed for me. I knew at a real gut level the importance of forming connections."

Tiye goes on to say: "Academia is so consuming. Besides teaching and doing research, I am asked to attend and assume responsibilities on all types of committees. I just can't do it all. Besides, I don't see the university as my whole life, yet it could be if I let it. I have many talents—theater, dance, painting pictures, sports, writing poems—and I like being involved in these other areas of my life. I commute to work, so that's a challenge too, and I've had to give up some things I really enjoy because I do commute."

Balance has become the biggest challenge for Tiye because of the many responsibilities in academia, others' expectations that she assume additional responsibilities, her many interests and talents, and the time lost by commuting.

"The university expectations are unreal. There is never a dull moment. It really is an impossible job—teaching; supervising; writing; advising; being on committees in the program, department, college, and university, being part of professional associations and professional development; conferences; presentations; editorial boards; grant writing; mentoring; service to the community. And then we're supposed to eat, sleep, attend to our families, go to the bathroom, and perhaps try to have a little recreation in there, too.

"When I first came here, White faculty seemed to have the expectation that I would automatically mentor and advise African American students in the program. So there I was mentoring and advising White students and all the students of color. I had to ask myself, 'Aren't all faculty responsible for the professional welfare and development of all students throughout the program?' This situation has changed now because I raised the issue. I don't think they realized the assumption that was being made, because when I finally spoke up about it they acted surprised.

"Also, African American students and other students of color place additional expectations on me. They expect me to be their mother, legal advisor, banker, counselor, and comrade, as well as their instructor. I think in many ways, as African American faculty, we have to be all of this, but when we don't live up to the expectation in students' eyes, then from their perspective we have really failed them.... I feel, at times, as though I have failed them."

Tiye handles the difficulties of academia and tries to bring balance to her life through sports, recreation, travel, and the arts. "At some level, I have to distance myself from all the demands and competitiveness of the university and ensure time for personal nurturance. For me it is in the form of dancing, piano, traveling, painting, playing tennis, gardening, swimming, or socializing with friends. You have to have a life outside the university that provides fun, relaxation, and validation of yourself. Being so busy ... is difficult, but I had to carve time to do this for myself. I just had to. Personal well-being is a high priority for me."

In responding to how she deals with racism and sexism, Tiye states, "I think it bothers me more when I see it happening to others rather than when it happens to me. Somehow, when racism or sexism hits me, I seem to work around it or things happen in such a way that I benefit in the long run. Spirit just takes over and something positive happens. For instance, one time I applied for a job and I didn't get it. I know the White boys were playing their games, and the brother of one of the board members was offered the job. Well, a few months later, I obtained ... a better job. Also, the people that hired the brother of this guy were later very disappointed in his performance. I received feedback from two board members who said they wished they had hired me, but by that time I had left the area for a better job. I had no control over it. It just happened.

"Several years ago, here at the university, I was on a search committee to select someone for an administrative position. After reviewing the paper work from all the applicants and interviewing the most promising candidates, it was very clear to me who the best candidate was. The experience of this candidate unequivocally stood above the rest. When it came time for the committee to discuss the candidates, the one I felt was the least qualified for the position was being discussed as the best candidate. The person I had chosen as the best qualified was at the bottom of mostly everyone else's list. I was astonished! I thought, 'What in the world! Did you all read the same paper work I did and interview the same candidates?' Anyway, the few committee members who originally were in agreement with me, I found out later, much later, after the search committee had finished its work, had received phone calls regarding their jobs being threatened. In the final vote, the person with the least qualifications won the vote and was offered the job. I was stunned. Somehow I thought righteousness would prevail somewhere in the process, but it didn't. Three months after the new person assumed the position, that person called the individual that I thought was the best candidate to say he was not familiar with the responsibilities of the position and needed help. I was so upset from having to serve on that committee; it actually affected my health for months. This was one of those situations where I had to turn it over to God and trust that in the long run righteousness still would prevail.

"As I reflect back, this was one of those situations where you begin to question yourself. A reality check would have been very helpful. But obtaining a reality check regarding racial issues from a trusted colleague is not always easy when we, as African Americans, are often isolated in our departments. That's why all of us sisters must stick together and help each other.

"Now, for my research I was fortunate because eventually a group of us sisters started meeting and supporting each other, providing reality checks for various situations we encountered along with enhancing our research agendas. We came from various program areas, started talking about issues we were facing, and realized the importance of us meeting on a regular basis. The upside of us getting together was that we supported each other. The downside was that we were all junior faculty at the time and really had no senior faculty to provide experienced insight.

"The university is very lonely. The demands are tremendous. I hardly have time to keep in contact with old friends. That keeps me even more isolated at times. I have no social life and feel like I have to really go out of my way to allow myself to have fun or socialize. Others who are not in this type of environment do not understand, and so there's this sort of distancing thing going on. It's not easy to respond to friends when I'm feeling so consumed, so some friends just sort of drifted away."

Tiye considers herself successful not because she has been tenured and promoted, but rather her feelings of success are derived from more altruistic goals. "Success for me is measured by the impact I have upon others, particularly long-term impact. In other words, have I made a positive difference in policy; social dynamics that contribute to the enhancement or empowerment of others, particularly people of color?

"I see research and writing as a means of impacting others, too. Through my writings, others gain perspectives that perhaps they had not considered before, or my writings help to clarify thoughts or feelings that others may have. My research is important, but it hasn't been easy. I work with a team of folks so we help each other out on papers. If I had to do it by myself, I don't think I would fare very well in research. It just takes so much time, and I don't have much time with so many responsibilities and expectations of me. With the team, some of us do the analyses, some write the purpose and theoretical perspectives of the article, we all critique and help to rewrite. We take turns being first author on the various articles. This process has helped a lot. Multiple authors on the projects has helped me to get many articles published. I only have a few single authored publications, which is looked upon more favorably by my colleagues. Nevertheless, this process [multiple authorship] has helped me not only to get published, but to become known among colleagues across the nation and even internationally in this line of research. I feel successful in that sense."

Amina

Although Amina, a full professor and the research administrator in the Black Studies Department has been successful in academia by academic standards, she has this to say about academia: "Academia, I think in general for anybody Black or White, is just vicious. It's too competitive, unnecessarily competitive. Competitiveness can be healthy, but academia is too competitive in a vicious, vindictive, underhanded way, and it affects entirely too many people. And there's so much work out there to do.... I have so many ideas by twelve o'clock in the afternoon, I can afford to give at least seventy-five percent of them away. So I can't figure out what everyone is fighting about."

In response to how this has affected her relationships, both positively and negatively, Amina says: "Full professorship has allowed me to operate at the level that my professors operated at, which is what I wanted to do. But on the other side, it has cost me. It has cost me sister friends because I won't get into male bashing. It has cost me male friends because I write about African women, which they usually think is an attack on males because they don't read it. In terms of scholarship, Whites say let them do this to keep them quiet; we don't want any more problems on campus. So there are no benefits there, either. You don't have a personal life. You're constantly at work. I've never taken a vacation and that's not healthy. I'm constantly in the struggle. I'm accountable. I feel so accountable all the time. That doesn't make people like you. If anything, it makes them dislike you. Distant. It's very lonely sometimes. I know an awful lot of people around the world that I've come in contact with, but there's not a lot of closeness. Part of it is fear, part is jealousy, and part ... is overwork. I don't have the time to socialize and develop and do those kinds of things that keep mind, body, and spirit together, and I think that's part of the problem with academia. It does not allow you to be a human being. Relationships and social interaction among humans is vital, and the university does not give one much opportunity for building that."

Other concerns Amina speaks of center around the perception of African American studies. "There is a lot of research and excitement ... regarding African American history, culture, relationships, etcetera, but unfortunately there are still many folks in academia who look upon this area of study as deficient in academic rigor. I want to change that perception. There is considerable academic rigor in what we do here.... Also, when I serve on committees regarding multicultural issues, these responsibilities are not given much credence when it comes to tenure or promotion considerations. When I write in journals regarding African American issues, these journals are not considered prestigious enough for promotion recommendations. I am a full professor now, but I've had to fight every inch of the way with people outside of the African American studies department. Because the research is sometimes new or provides a different perspective than traditionally, because it is based on a different population, even publishing companies will question and challenge the writing, causing a longer time to get published.

"I've had to fight to keep the African American Studies programs going. If there are going to be budget cuts, this program is often looked at as one to go. That wouldn't happen with the literature program or psychology program. It has been a struggle all along the way."

What keeps Amina going? "In some ways I've had opportunities and exposure to many things, and I want African American youth to experience some of these same things and even more. Also, I tell myself that there are a lot of Black people who died for me to be here. I tell myself that if spirit didn't have something for me to do, that I would not have been privileged to have all this exposure, and known all these people, and listened to these lectures, and traveled up and down West Africa with fifty dollars in my pocket. I have an obligation that when I die I want to be able to die peacefully, knowing that I did the best I could with what I had. What keeps me going? I've got three kids and two grandchildren, and I want them to say, you know, my momma kicked butt and took none of this. If they can say that, then I'm going to be a happy camper. They'll say she didn't always bake us cookies, but she did kick butt and took none of this."

Analysis

The stories shared by these women certainly validate research on the issues that African American women face in PWIs. The following themes have been identified in the women's comments. Statements of the women were coded, and those with similar content or focus were categorized together, resulting in three major themes. The three themes were (1) joys of academia, (2) obstacles and struggles, and (3) coping strategies for survival and success in academia. In this chapter we discuss the first two themes.

Joys of Academia

Categories within the first theme include (A) utilization of skills and abilities, (B) autonomy, (C) helping others, (D) leadership, (E) exploration and advancement of new ideas, and (F) status as a faculty member or administrator.

Utilization of skills and abilities. The women enjoy the opportunity to utilize their skills and talents for their profession within the university system. The university provides a setting whereby intellectual discourse is constant for these very intelligent and talented women. Tiye remembers that as a child, her family often enjoyed sitting at the dinner table discussing all kinds of ideas and issues. She notes that the university setting is like being at the dinner table; it is a place where ideas and issues can be created, explored, examined, analyzed, and challenged. The women relish this type of experience. Nzingha remarkes, "There are work settings where innovation and creative ideas are not encouraged. Here they are welcomed."

Autonomy. The women enjoy the autonomy they experience at work. They speak of being able to explore their own areas of research, to set their own schedules for teaching classes and advising students, and to make decisions about their involvement in academic and professional activities. They comment that autonomy increases as one moves up in rank but note that in general the university offers considerable autonomy. While they appreciate the importance of collaborative collegial endeavors, they also appreciate the greater freedom they have in not having to answer to superiors. They all note that it would be difficult to return to a position where everything you do is watched and supervised by someone after having functioned so long without such oversight. Cleopatra notes, "I love being able to function, think, and make decisions on this level—a colleague level—and not have some superior over me telling me what I can or cannot do.... being treated as a child as if I would be irresponsible. I have friends who work in companies like that and I don't think I would be able to stand it." Being able to make important decisions regarding career, profession, family, and life is important to these women. These are women who have a strong desire to manage their own destiny, and the university system affords them the opportunity to do so. The women gain satisfaction from having the control and freedom they lacked in other settings. The autonomy reinforces their confidence. With such autonomy, they are free to be themselves and to go after the things that are important to them.

Helping others. For all of the study participants, the highlight of their relationships within the university is their interaction with students. They enjoy being able to make significant contributions to students and find much satisfaction in being a part of their growth and development. They all acknowledge a commitment to the assistance, guidance, and mentorship, particularly of African American students. African Americans are often raised with the notion that the skills and abilities they obtain should contribute to the general welfare of the Black community and that they are "mechanisms for social and institutional change" (Edwards and Camblin, 1998, p. 33; see also Staples and Johnson, 1995). Serving the community is often stated as a primary objective among many African Americans in any field of work. Staples and Johnson (1995) stated that Black female college students entering nontraditional fields did so because of a strong drive to serve the needs of Black people. They also stated that satisfaction among Black men and women derived from contributing to the general welfare of the Black community and supporting and nurturing their families. Achieving these ends outweighed any negative effect of performing multiple roles. The contribution these women perceive they are making to the community is not only important, but it is also the primary motivation that keeps them in the university setting. Community is a salient value of many people of African descent.

Leadership. The women enjoy being in leadership positions where what they do and say make a positive difference in the university and in their profession. Leadership offers them a sense of control over their destiny and satisfaction because the decisions they make impact students and their profession positively. Nzingha notes that being a Black woman in leadership refutes negative stereotypes of African American women, demonstrating that they can think and act professionally, doing more than making babies and receiving welfare checks.

Exploration and advancement of new ideas. These women enjoy exploring new ideas. They are inquisitive and investigative. They enjoy researching, thereby contributing to their professions as well as to humanity and to knowledge. Cleopatra believes that "Research should contribute to liberation, freedom, and empowerment." Tiye says, "I love researching, exploring, finding out things and creating new ideas and ways of looking at things. It's exciting and keeps me going. However, the research should contribute to something, such as helping people to better their lives." All five of the women describe their thirst for knowledge and their immersion into exploring new ideas as exuberating and equate it to a natural high for them.

Status as a faculty member or administrator. The women enjoy the status and the respect they receive as a faculty member or an administrator. There is a level of prestige that comes with identifying oneself as a university administrator or faculty person. As African American women, they note the numerous places and situations throughout their lives where they had received little respect because of their gender, class, or race, but they see how the reactions of others change immediately when it becomes known what they do in the academy. Suddenly they are afforded greater respect. "It's a shame it has to be that way, but it is reality.... Even those who would like to cut my throat and stomp me in the ground can't deny that I have a lot goin' on, so they back off and provide some degree of respect. I like standing tall and being respected; anyone would," says Nzingha. For African American women who have historically been viewed with little respect, such a position is a welcome opportunity.

In summary, the study participants have a community in which autonomy and creativity are highly prized and can thus see opportunities for sharing their gifts for the benefit of others. Bringing their gifts to the table, however, is not without its hardships. Each of the women speak of the obstacles and hurts they endure.

Obstacles and Struggles

The second theme is obstacles and struggles. Eight categories have been identified. These include: (A) institutional oppression; (B) over-scrutinization by peers, superiors, and students; (C) challenge to professional knowledge and experience; (D) friction between cultural orientation and university orientation; (E) role overload; (F) lack of support for goals; (G) lack of professional support systems; and (H) exclusion from the informal network system.

Institutional oppression. Our participants have a lot to say about the institutional oppression they experience. In particular, they speak of being in an environment that is not always validating. It appears that, for the most part, these women do not feel fully accepted and integrated into the university community, in spite of their expertise. They note a general feeling of being disconnected and marginalized, primarily because they are Black and female. For most of the women, a great deal of effort was put forth to hire them, but since they have arrived in their departments, they are mostly left to function without much direction or guidance. Colleagues are rarely open to engaging collaboratively in research with them. While this exclusion is not always seen as deliberate, the women note how colleagues do not even consider them as research and writing partners. At a very fundamental level, the women share with us how important it is to be valued and validated in the community in which they have chosen to do their life's work and how heartbreaking it is not to experience this in academia.

The women describe prejudicial attitudes and institutional racism in academia as pervasive, intense and deeply ingrained in the culture of the institution. In some cases they are evaluated for tenure and promotion by a set of criteria different than that by which their colleagues are judged. For example, student and peer evaluations are often based on negative racial assumptions rather than performance. In some cases the expectation to be a team player often means pressure to overlook discriminatory practices. If discriminatory practices are pointed out, then one is seen as uncooperative. They speak of colleagues who assume that they will not perform well in research activities and then provide little support to help them to succeed. The bias that colleagues hold (cannot perform well) feed their behavior (no support), making it difficult to discredit the bias that has already been formed. Some colleagues assume that because their colleague is an African American woman, she can have no agenda but to fulfill whatever White males want. "When I informed my colleagues of my research agenda, they acted very surprised," explains Nzingha. Furthermore, the women talk about how their research areas are not highly valued by their colleagues. "When you have little support, colleagues who do not value your area of research, numerous responsibilities, and time constraints, it's easy to get discouraged about your research agenda," explains Tiye. Cleopatra and Amina, as administrators, note how subordinates sometimes even despise following instructions or receiving constructive criticisms simply because an African American woman is in charge.

None of our participants have been able to escape the harsh sting and humiliation of institutional racism, regardless of her position, rank, institution, or perceived power. They see themselves 'jumping through hoops' – explaining, justifying, educating, challenging - that are not required of colleagues.

Compounding the race issue, sexism is also woven into the institutional fabric and makes for an uncomfortable, if not "chilly," environment for these women. While other women may experience sexism, African American women encounter specific issues related to the fact they are African American as well as women. Sexism appears to be as much concerned with attitudes as with behavior. For example, one woman reports the concern about being asked to solve problems or accept tasks that the others (usually White males) have either abandoned, cannot solve, or do not want. We have coined the phrase "the clean-up woman syndrome." In her book *Sister Power*, Patricia Reid-Merritt quotes a woman who aptly said, "A Black woman doesn't get to be mayor of a big city until it's bankrupt." Another woman uses a different analogy: "If a ship is about to sink, then call in a Black woman to save it."

Over-scrutinization by peers, superiors, and students. Over-scrutinization is another shared experience of the women. African American women have to work harder, be smarter, and be super competent in order to make it in the academic environment. They cannot make the same mistakes that their White counterparts make and expect to be forgiven or to get ahead. There is a feeling that someone is always looking over their shoulders, criticizing their work, their leadership style, and expecting failure. This may also be related to an assumption that an African American woman obtained her position because she is Black and female, and thus she is an affirmative action hire who is unqualified for the position.

Challenge to professional knowledge and experience. All five of the participants report that their competence and knowledge are challenged and questioned. This factor is related to the point that African American women are viewed as the "other" and therefore intellectually inferior. They talk about students who challenge what and how these women teach, as well as about colleagues who question the purposes and rationale of their teaching. As a Black woman, there is a sense that your competence and knowledge are always up for question. This is the "if you're a Black woman, you can't possibly know what you're talking about" syndrome. This is also related to the academy's general perception that research regarding people of color is not legitimate or worthwhile scholarship unless it is conducted by Whites.

Friction between cultural orientation and university orientation. Friction between participants' original learning and developmental environment and the institutional environment is evident. These are women who benefited from unconditional love and respect. Being accepted was a given in their childhood or in their African American communities. We learn from the women that being valued and having a sense of belonging in the community are extremely important. Nandi notes, "We were around well-to-do people, but I was accepted and never felt diminished by that even though we were financially impoverished." In the PWI setting, however, the women are not readily valued as individuals. Several of the participants feel a dissonance between their cultural world view and the university's world view. Considering the pervasiveness of racism and sexism in the academy, it is difficult for African American women to be validated and accepted. When comparing a predominantly White institution to a community college with a large African American population Cleopatra states, "The climate is definitely different at this institution. It was like moving from a warm climate to a cool one. And, there was a definite chill in the air.

The women note how their more collaborative, cooperative worldview and means of accomplishing goals is different from and not as highly valued as the university's individualistic, competitive worldview and means of accomplishing goals. Nzingha notes, "It seems like everyone is always fighting each other to get things done instead of taking time to see how they might work together. Our department had already identified several issues that needed to be addressed, so I presented an idea to develop and implement what I thought would be an innovative program that would benefit students. I sought support from colleagues to provide input and assist in the effort. Immediately, I received flack from colleagues who expressed all kinds of reasons why it wouldn't work; who tried to put forth their own programs; and who, most heartbreakingly, attempted to put me down by questioning my competency and my intentions. This was so frustrating, when all I wanted to do was serve students and all I had done was request a collaborative effort from colleagues. It was like a war; everyone was out for himself/herself and downgrading others to do so. It just didn't make sense to me."

Amina mentions, "Not having the time to socialize and develop and do those kinds of things that keep mind, body, and spirit together, ... I think that's part of the problem with academia. It does not allow you to be a human being."

Role overload. A major concern of the participants is the numerous responsibilities that are expected of them beyond their contractual responsibilities. With teaching, advising, mentoring, researching, writing, presenting, being on committees, as well as maintaining non-university responsibilities, they feel fragmented. They note the difficulty of managing all their roles and the detrimental impact this has on their families and personal lives. They talk about being expected to assume roles that other faculty are not expected to assume, such as being the sole voice for diversity issues or African American students. They are often asked to be representatives on numerous committees. African American women are said to be the most overworked of all faculty in academe (Graves, 1990; Gregory, 1995; Peterson, 1990). Role overload is confusing because the women feel service is important and they want to serve, but they also feel overwhelmed. The demands placed on them—more courses to teach, more students to advise/mentor, more committees on which to serve—often result in the loss of friendships, poor health, scattered professional direction and goals, unproductive research, and considerable stress. With such high demands, nurturing relationships becomes nearly impossible. Thus the women feel a separation of mind, body, and spirit.

Tiye states, "There is a high expectation among university leaders for African Americans to serve in many ways. I can understand that because sometimes they want to bring us to the table and hear our voice. That is important. Yet, as an individual, I cannot serve on all the committees I'm asked to serve and remain healthy. As an individual one has to find balance. As a group, we can perhaps distribute our service throughout the university." The other women agree that they need to more effectively prioritize and determine what is most important.

Lack of support for goals. Nandi notes, "A lot of looks and stares come up when I talk about my research on African Americans. Because many White colleagues don't understand it and hold biased assumptions, they do not value African American research as highly." Nzingha adds, "Since I've always held the perspective that education and research are for liberation, it is important that I keep my focus there. Considering our collective history, it makes sense to focus our energies on such an agenda. But why colleagues consider my research on African Americans as of less value is simply prejudicial." Unfortunately, there exists a general perception in the academy that research on people of color is not legitimate scholarship. This fact results in limited research partnerships for African American women.

As Tiye expresses, "The competitiveness was difficult to deal with. Whereas there were times I wanted to work with colleagues in a collaborative way, they were content to function alone. Throughout the university, people talked about working collaboratively—it's one of the university's goals—yet the reality was that faculty typically didn't do it. Whenever a small group attempted to function collaboratively, they were seen by others as wasting valuable time discussing and not getting things done. Sometimes they were seen as weak, unfocused, or indecisive. The system does not value or reward collaboration; it upholds uniqueness, distinctive competency, the expert. So everyone is out to make a name for him or herself. Everyone wants his or her own personal credit."

Lack of professional support systems. Another shared experience of the study participants is their lack of professional support systems. As a researcher, Sheila Gregory (1995) has pointed out that, in an academic setting, supportive networks and hospitable environments are particularly important for African American faculty women, who often seek various types of professional, social, and religious networks. These networks provide a source of support, strength, and encouragement to help people to persevere in an often stressful and competitive academic environment. Nevertheless, in some cases these women are the only persons of color in their units, and in a few cases they are even the first. They feel isolated with no visible support from their departmental colleagues. They usually have no one to assist them in learning the institutional politics, especially with regard to learning the pathway to the rewards of promotion and tenure.

Nzingha states, "Another African American colleague told me to write down everything I do and try to balance service, teaching, and research. I followed his advice, although I wasn't sure how to balance service, teaching, and research, but, when it came time for the tenure and promotion process, I just wrote down everything I did. It worked. I was lucky. No one else had given me any direction as to how to submit my materials. While that was helpful, I couldn't help but feel that it was more than just my record of activities that landed me my tenure and promotion. There was an unsaid social or relationship component. I think many of my colleagues liked my friendliness and perhaps misread my congenial nature as lacking agendas that would conflict or challenge their perspectives. There's always this social and political stuff going on."

Nandi explains, "Having a mentor early on to give some direction and to sort of take you under his or her wing—to protect you, in a sense, to keep you from overloading yourself from requests to do this and that—would have been very helpful when I was first starting. My colleagues like me and so they were supportive in providing general information at times, but the specifics of what I was to do or not do was missing. Should I take on this assignment or that assignment? Is it better to serve in the department or outside the department? What is a reasonable load of advisees? How many publications? I was very observant and noticed that those who were more successful were those who were focused in one area of inquiry and practice. So I began to do that myself, and that helped. But it took me a long time to figure that out on my own."

The publication process was an area that initially brought a lot of stress to the women. Tiye states, "Publication is expected, but little direction or guidance is provided in making it happen. When I first came to the university, I was expected to write grants for research and to publish papers regarding research, and yet no one ever spoke with me or provided any mentorship regarding carving out a research area, grant writing, or the process of getting a paper published. I learned through trial and error on my own and a lot of perseverance and that is why I am where I am today—dogged determination in spite of everything. Certain things that publishers expected for submission of papers ... well if I had had some guidance, I probably could have saved a lot of time and heartaches if someone had shared with me what sort of things to expect from publishers."

Amina notes, "Research and writing papers for publication requires a lot of time. I mean a lot of time—research time, thinking time, writing time. With all the responsibilities we have, it is impossible to find enough time to do adequate research. We are on overload because we are expected to do so much more than our colleagues—serving on committees in the department and university, helping out in the community, having an outrageous number of students to advise, teaching more courses than colleagues. It's vicious."

Several of the women have not felt supported by other persons of color on campus. Cleopatra exclaims, "What is more painful is that some of our own people work against us. Nzingha adds to this: "Why we fight among each other over hamburger is beyond me when we can work together for the steak. Deep inside, some of us must not believe we can have steak."

Internalized oppression is an area of concern noted by some of the women. Systematic, institutionalized oppression of people—in other words, external oppression—causes an internalized oppression for its victims such that they are physically, emotionally, and spiritually battered. They are oppressed to the point that they begin to believe their oppression is deserved, natural, and merely their lot in life; they become angry or bitter toward people of their own cultural, racial, or ethnic background. While sometimes shaken as a result of oppressive experiences that challenge their personhood and their sense of value as human beings, these five women refuse to internalize the oppression. Since understanding the dynamics of oppression, they have been able to identify it for what it is and to recognize the beauty and value of who they are.

All of the women talk about the political dynamics that occur in their departments. These situations are especially difficult without an experienced colleague who can provide perspective and advice. They note how racism and sexism are often covert, making them hard to identify. The lack of professional support often leaves African American women void of information necessary for their continued success and sometimes leaves them confused and uncertain about the situations they see. Collegial support can go a long way in helping African American women to obtain reality checks about their experiences and to combat their confusion and self-doubt.

Exclusion from the informal network system. Unwritten rules and practices and informal conversations are noted as being both frustrating and confusing. Tiye notes, "A lot of sharing through informal conversations and networks occurs in the department to which I am not privy. Then when I attend a department or program meeting where I may provide input or even ask a question, there are looks and stares and comments made that are totally unexpected or confusing. I feel like I've missed something. I may find out later that I had been left totally in the dark because of certain assumptions, expectations, or decisions that my colleagues had already made through their informal conversations held earlier."

Tiye also states, "When I first came to the university, my colleagues often went out to lunch together. I noticed that I was never invited. Finally, one day I said, 'I would like to go to lunch with you,' and a couple of them looked so surprised. I wasn't sure if they were surprised I asked or surprised that I like to eat too. One of the women came up to me the next day and said she was sorry I had not been asked to go to lunch with them and that she just didn't think to ask. So often we just become invisible."

They are sometimes left out of important discussions where decisions have negative consequences for them. The women speak of how information is often passed along to or decisions made with colleagues without their inclusion. More importantly, being left out or ignored, they feel invisible. Whether the exclusion is intentional or not, the result is the same. Imagine living in a home with other family members, but you are treated as an invisible entity. That is devastating to one's functioning as well as to one's psychological and emotional well being.

Summary

We see that these five women enjoy being in the university setting and believe that they have a divine purpose for being there. They speak passionately about their gifts, what they offer in the academic setting, and their hopes for students. They confirm their joy in working with students, teaching, and attending to professional activities. While the women have had many positive experiences in academia, they also experience numerous obstacles and challenges. They speak of times in which they have received validation from colleagues, but they feel that these experiences are few and far between. They lament the fact that there is not more closeness with colleagues in general, and with African American colleagues in particular, and sometimes feel alienated from them. Raised in communities that loved, affirmed, and valued them, now each of the women speaks of academia as a setting that does not value their essence. The women do not readily find a strong sense of community in academia. Further, we see that racism figures prominently in creating this lack of community. Racism serves as a barrier to full inclusion, and, therefore, the women are not effectively acknowledged and affirmed by the university. In short, these women bring their gifts to the university community and, too often, what they bring is not truly valued.

In his text, *The Healing Wisdom of Africa*, Malidoma Patrice Somé (1998) speaks eloquently and profoundly about the importance of community. He writes: "The community thus takes upon itself the responsibility of nurturing and protecting the individual because the individual knowing her or his purpose will then invest energy in sustaining the community." What happens when the individual is not fully engaged and sustained by the community? Somé (1998) revealed that "community is vital and the need to be acknowledged by the community is so primal that if it does not happen in the village, town or neighborhood, people will go out searching for it." Essentially, lack of acknowledgement in the community results in rejection, isolation, and, in many instances, withdrawal from that community.

The five women speak about the ills of institutional racism and sexism and give vivid descriptions of oppressive situations. They discuss the disconnect they see between their cultural world view and the traditional university practices and expectations. Whereas the university traditionally emphasizes and honors individual accomplishments, our study participants note positive aspects of collaborative work. While collaboration has been more recently emphasized in university mission statements, the reality is that individualism is still highly prized. They discuss the isolation that is often felt in their departments. The women also note that their holistic manner of functioning, particularly in the classroom, often raises suspicion from colleagues, as well as from students. The women find that the diversity of gifts which they often bring to the setting is not highly regarded or respected. While diversity is said to be important, there are long held perspectives, which restrict other perspectives, of what is considered to be appropriate in the academic setting.

Nevertheless, all five of the women are highly motivated to withstand the issues of the university because of their drive to make a difference in their professions and in the lives of students. The voices of the five women in our study suggest that collective efforts are necessary and that it is indeed the collective responsibility (ujima) of both Black and White professionals to create an environment of collaboration and to combat oppressive conditions (e.g. racism, sexism) in any of their manifestations.

CHAPTER 4
Ujamaa
Coping

I'm like a tree planted by the rivers of the water. I shall not be moved. Stay and claim that which is your own.

When we capitalize upon our collective resources (ujamaa—cooperative economics) and work together we can claim that which is our own and move mountains. Usually when we think of economics we think of money. Money, however, is a resource for obtaining things we need or desire. Ujamaa, in the context of this chapter, refers to the personal and social resources at our disposal that allow us to obtain those things we need and desire. Personal resources include the characteristics individuals possess (e.g., self-esteem, attitude, education, wealth, motivation). Social resources are the relationships individuals possess (e.g., family, relatives, friends). This chapter examines the third theme, coping strategies, through personal and social resources. We learn how the women effectively deal with the challenges they encounter in academia. We learn also about their means of working collaboratively with others to make a difference.

Seven main categories of coping resources that the women utilize have been identified. The first category centers upon relationships and support. This finding supports research showing that job satisfaction among female faculty is strongly related to personal interactions (Robertson and Bean, 1998) and the quality of their relationships (Josephs, Markus, and Tafarodi, 1992). It also supports a self-in-relation theory that posits women's core self-structure, or their primary motivational thrust as concerning growth within relationships, showing that connection with others is a key component of action and growth (Drummond, 1997). The second category focuses on the humanistic values the women hold and is described within two sub-categories. The third category centers upon knowledge and understanding of university dynamics and expectations and the acquisition of allies. It is described within three sub-categories. Having the know-how of tenure, promotion, merit pay, department and university service, and interaction dynamics among colleagues is necessary for successful engagement of the university setting. The fourth category focuses on psychological resources and is discussed within five sub-categories. The fifth category focuses on emotional intelligence. The sixth category focuses on spiritual resources and is discussed within two sub-categories. Cognitive skills, emotional maturity, and spiritual beliefs have been found in other research as factors for effective coping (Bjorck and Cohen, 1993; Hathaway and Pargament, 1992; Williams, etc., 2006). The seventh category explores the women's challenge to oppression.

Relationships and Support

All of the participants talk about relying on a supportive figure during hurtful and difficult challenges to their work, identity, and integrity. In some cases, supportive and understanding colleagues are the ones they can talk to and from whom they can gain support. In other cases it is family members, friends, or students. Having strong family, friend, community, or collegial support is extremely important and the five study participants utilize all these support systems. All of the women emphasize the importance of the support and encouragement they receive from family, both immediate and extended. This support is evident from early childhood through adulthood and is instrumental in helping the women feel confident that they can achieve their goals. Some of the women grew up in intact families and some did not. Nevertheless, they all acknowledge the fact that life does not have to be perfect for adults to spend time with their children.

The women also talk about the encouragement they receive from older African American women in the community as well as from ministers, neighbors, teachers, and friends of their relatives. The many people who believe in them, shower them with attention, and essentially tell them "you're smart and you can do whatever you set out to do" significantly enhance the confidence of these women. High expectations were common messages within the childhood communities of these women. These five women grew up knowing that others believed in them and that they could do exceedingly well in spite of any adversities they may encounter. They have had numerous experiences that gave them confidence in their abilities. These connections are a constant source of strength for the women and come about through shared informal conversations where everyone values each other and shares in each others' lives. The people in these women's lives provide a firm foundation and stimulate an inner voice within them, a voice that arises from the positive aspects of their childhood environments and enables them to believe in themselves.

Having had a rich background of support in their early years, these women speak of the loneliness, frustration, and isolation they feel in their academic departments. This often results in confusion and feelings of rejection, helplessness, uncertainty, and doubt. At times, they doubt their own experiences and worth. But these feelings are short-lived when countered by encouragement from their support system to be themselves and to stay true to themselves. Thus having support in the university is extremely important to them.

Strong Humanistic Values and Goals

Desire to Assist and Be with Students

Regardless of any difficult issues with which the women have contended one thing that keeps them going is their desire to work with and to help students. Supportive, growth-producing interactions with students are cherished by these five successful women. Realizing the lack of support for many students of color in academia, these women feel especially committed to assisting them and even express a sense of guilt when they are not able to be there for them. Tiye and Cleopatra note that when they place their focus on assisting students, they are better able to face whatever academic hardships they may personally encounter. "Sometimes in my active involvement to help students, I forget or put aside the unfairness that I may be experiencing because I believe I need to be there for the students," says Tiye.

Furthermore, by facing the challenges, the women believe they can assist students to feel more empowered. "Our sacrifices for students sometimes bring on changes in the institution that enable students to be more empowered," notes Cleopatra. Tiye says, "I remember one time a fight broke out at an undergraduate fraternity party. The university wanted to ban all parties of African Americans or subject them to security checks at their parties. We—African American administrators, faculty, and students—challenged the university regarding their intentions. The whole affair was kind of nasty. I was the spokesperson, but we were all outspoken and appalled that the university wanted to take such action. It was discriminatory. Besides, the students that were fighting were not even from our university. Finally the university abandoned its intentions, and I felt good about my role in fighting for the students." These experiences conjure up a fighting spirit and enable the women to cope with obstacles and challenges.

Contribution to the Profession

Knowing that your actions are for the benefit and good of others helps one to deal with oppressive situations. By contributing to their professions, these five phenomenal women are able not only to stand guard for students, but also to bring new and helpful information to many others. This provides the women with a sense of accomplishment. "Publishing articles that focus on injustices in the profession is rewarding and fulfilling for me," explains Tiye. "It's helping the profession get its act together while providing a voice for the many people the profession is serving." "Also," Amina notes, "knowing that you are helping to bring new knowledge and understanding within your profession is very gratifying. Knowing that I am enhancing a program that will benefit so many people is personally rewarding."

Knowledge and Understanding of University Dynamics and Expectations

Research, Service, Teaching

All of the women talk about the importance of knowing and understanding university—and in particular departmental—expectations for research, service, and teaching, as well as what is required for tenure, promotion, and merit pay. While the women express some of their initial confusion and misunderstanding regarding these processes, they note that such understanding is critical to success in the academy. Considering that Nandi, Tiye, and Nzingha indicate that they have had some general instruction regarding these processes, they note the absence of guidance specific to their needs and concerns. Looking back, they believe that mentorship would have assisted them in progressing more quickly. Two of the study participants note that their enthusiasm and passion for their profession is what help them move through the tenure and promotion process. They say they had an abundance of energy that they directed to addressing professional issues, and this led them to attain tenure and promotion. Tiye states, "You know, I didn't even think about or focus on the tenure and promotion process. I just did the things I enjoyed and wanted to do. When it came time for tenure and promotion, I had what was necessary." She also states, "I kept records of everything I did so that my file would be complete for promotion."

The other women see the process as confusing and filled with uncertainty. Nzingha states, "I tell junior faculty to ask questions and obtain as much specific information as possible. When I went through the process, I wasn't sure what colleagues were looking for. I knew what they wanted on the surface. Sure they want you to teach, provide service, and mostly do research, but there is always something else they want that goes unsaid. No one is ever specific about how much service, teaching, or research is necessary or the quality that is required. As I look back, I think for tenure they were also looking for a person that would be a good 'fit;' compatible. Collegiality is very important. For me, I think they were looking for someone not too militant or different in his/her thinking. This is difficult for some African Americans who may be very bold in speaking out about injustices they see. If you're seen as a trouble maker, it's all over. There's this bit of conflict between being true to self and moving up in your career. In some departments it may not be as difficult as in others, so it varies, but it's a reality that is experienced by many of us. And of course, if you're a woman, the expectation is that you don't speak out at all. So how we act as African American women may counter colleagues' ideas of how a woman is to function, and some African American women are not going to hold back or compromise themselves in that way. This makes the tenure and promotion process more complex. I know I came across sort of militant. But I could always provide evidence for what I had to say and took action while displaying respect and integrity, so few could dispute that. They may have been afraid not to give me tenure. (Laughing.)"

What three of the women express is the balance they have to manage between being themselves and meeting the university's expectations. "I love doing a lot of different things and helping out. That's my nature. But I had to realize that being expected to help in the university was wearing me out and hindering my research efforts. It helps and is important to be known in the university setting, but I had to get focused on my research agenda. I enjoy teaching and service, but it is important to not delay your research." explains Tiye.

All the women, however, express the complexity that their gender and race add to obtaining promotion. "Those reviewing our articles about African Americans and women often do not understand our research, so sometimes it gets turned down or you have to spend weeks or months trying to explain to the reviewers what your research is really about and why you did it the way you did. It gets crazy," notes Amina.

"When I saw the respect that students and colleagues were giving to professors that had publications, I knew that I must get busy and write," says Nandi. Amina initially struggled with publishing: "I found it hard to keep submitting articles and having them turned down. It's just so disheartening after you've put so much work into it. I think what got me over the hump was dogged determination and collaboration of research with colleagues who provided encouragement and affirmed that what I was writing about was important."

The women enjoy the rewards of tenure and promotion, such as higher salaries, favorable work schedules, job security, and the ability to better assist students and contribute their thoughts and ideas to their discipline. They also acknowledge the spoken and unspoken aspects of obtaining tenure and promotion and believe it is important to ask questions and solicit the help of senior faculty to aid in the process. Nzingha also states, "When things don't go well and you don't get tenured or promoted, simply readjust, obtain more specifics, and try again. Some departments require book contracts, complete manuscripts, a certain or vague number of articles published, outside letters from colleagues, teaching evaluations. It varies, so ask and obtain as much direction as possible."

Informal Network

The women speak of political dynamics among colleagues within departments. They affirm the importance of understanding informal leadership lines and issues among colleagues. Tiye states, "I found it interesting that the chair of the department would give direction about certain things, and before one could turn around good, another whole focus or agenda would take place. This would leave me very confused. Then I began to note how I had been left out of additional conversations that had taken place. Since I wasn't privy to those conversations, I would wonder what happened. How did everything get changed? Did I miss something? It was pretty confusing! Then I'd sit there and feel stupid. I noted on several occasions that sometimes, after a meeting, two or three of the junior faculty would get together with one of the senior male faculty, discuss the issues, and then follow the lead of the senior male faculty, even if it countered the chairperson."

The women gradually came to learn such dynamics by listening and speaking with others. However, this particular learning is made more difficult because, as African American women, they are often left out of informal conversations. As Nandi notes, "I initially took it as something personal, like maybe I neglected to hear something in the meeting or that I forgot something, or maybe I didn't understand totally what was meant. I assumed it was my fault. But then I began taking 'serious' notes and realized it wasn't me. My colleagues had changed something and I was left out of the loop." They find themselves having to challenge this practice. The women note that if they had had a well informed and knowledgeable mentor, they might have been able to negotiate the system more easily. "Learning the ropes and who is really in charge of things is critical," notes Amina. "I don't know how anyone would survive in this environment without this knowledge. I had no assistance here, so I just had to be assertive and a bit invasive to find out what was important. Not everyone is going to be as pushy as I. But my advice is that you need a good mentor or to get pushy ... or be very observant and consider the fact that informal conversations are happening."

It is clear from the women's voices that African American women must acknowledge that there is an informal network, that conversations exist without their inclusion, and that they must confront and challenge changes in information that appear confusing or different than what was previously presented.

Acquisition of Allies

There will be people who believe as you do, have similar goals, and function in similar ways. All five women state that this is most important for their retention at their respective universities. "Without a few allies, I would have never made it here," exclaims Nandi. "The university is a lonely and competitive world. Without some supporters and colleagues operating as I do, I would not be here," notes Amina.

Nzingha states, "Without a formal mentorship program, acquiring allies is important. Allies can serve somewhat in a mentorship role. As African American women, we seldom have mentors, which I think stems from the stereotype that we can handle things. When we do, it is typically a cross-gender mentor relationship. There are neither enough women nor African Americans. So the cross-gender mentor, that in itself can be problematic due to negative attitudes men may have regarding women's competencies, let alone their attitudes about African Americans. Some male mentors are too overprotective, taking on a patriarchal and very patronizing role. Then there are the assumptions others may make about the relationship, suggesting sexual overtones in the relationship when the one being mentored is simply trying to learn and do her professional best. If you're lucky, you might get a good mentor, and there are some. I just watched others and gradually learned, but without a mentor it probably took me longer. So having allies is good. They will work along side you because you have common beliefs and goals. Without allies, I don't think I would have made it this far." Nzingha goes on to say, "As one example, directing a dissertation takes a lot of skill and political savvy. There are numerous issues that arise. Just knowing there is someone you can talk to regarding the intricacies of directing the dissertation can be helpful."

Tiye states, "The primary thing that gave me strength was discussions with others who were going through the same things I was going through. I would feel all alone, asking myself what's wrong with me and thinking I was the only one going through this. But when I realized others were having the same experiences and feelings, I felt the connection and felt stronger." For these women, their motivation to succeed in the university setting increases as they come to understand collectively and historically and as they make connections with others.

Amina points out, "Allies are important, yet being seen as a person who is able to work independently is important too. You don't want to be seen as needy and dependent, so you want to connect with others and acquire allies and yet demonstrate independent thinking and functioning. There is a balance to achieve here. So I work with others, but I initiate many of my own ideas. I try to be a follower at times and I demonstrate leadership." They acknowledge that the acquisition of allies in the university system helps them in their academic success.

Cleopatra, Tiye, and Nzingha talk about how they eventually obtained support in their research endeavors. However, they state that their support initially did not come from colleagues within their departments. Even after years of writing in professional journals, Tiye states that none of the colleagues in her department have ever asked about writing with her, although she has told them she would be open to doing so. Nzingha says some of her support is from colleagues within the university, but not from colleagues in her department. Her support comes also from colleagues at other universities whom she met through professional organizations or working on professional issues. As an administrator Cleopatra has no time for research but works with other faculty when she can to do some writing. They all emphasize that support is important and necessary in fulfilling research objectives. Whether for research, everyday functioning, or committee projects, these women see the importance of engaging in relationships with colleagues who hold similar beliefs. Summarizing the statements of the five women, Tiye reiterates, "With so many obligations, it's difficult enough to maintain a research agenda, so having colleagues who will engage in the same research area as you and work together on projects, writing, committees, and department and program objectives is the best way to manage."

Psychological Resources

Belief in Self

Having a history of support and personal validation from childhood, these women are confident in their personal skill and abilities. They have had numerous experiences that have helped to build a strong sense of self-efficacy. Arising from nurturing and caring communities, the five women developed characteristics that enable them to succeed. Others encourage and believe in them. Through their experiences the women find power within themselves to excel.

These women have developed a stubbornness that does not permit them to sway from what they believe is important and right. Often the price for holding steadfast is high, but these women have learned to illustrate in their behavior the integrity and honor held by their parents, relatives, and other adults in their communities. They have learned that in order to build good and effective communities, they must indeed be courageous. They had learned to persevere even in the midst of pain and criticism. Their rich background of support enables them to do so. The wisdom and strength of character held by others has been instilled in them.

These women believe in themselves because they are well educated. They take full advantage of the schooling they have had and the opportunities that have been offered to them throughout their lives and know they have the intellect to achieve their goals.

Their belief in themselves is also strengthened by their strong ethnic identities. As they journey along their life path, they are connected to their own people. Stories of the experiences and traditions of relatives and friends imparted a deep sense of family heritage, ethnic identity, and pride. Some of the women knew their Black history and the sociopolitical dynamics of being Black in this society and the world from an early age and some did not. However, those who did not eventually came to learn about this and now recognize it as a powerful framework for understanding their experiences. While contextualizing the issues proves an ongoing struggle in their attempt to achieve a sense of wholeness, they rely on allies to help them separate what is personal from what is contextual and to resist the internalization of oppression. They know what it is like to be in a system that attempts to make Black women less than what they are, and they have learned not to succumb to it. They all too often experience the pain their ancestors and forbearers experienced when others tried to make them feel inferior. Yet as some of their forbearers rebuked this notion, so too have these five phenomenal women.

High Achievement Needs

These are women with high achievement needs and an internal locus of control. They explore, ask questions, and investigate and then find alternative ways to reach their goals. Their passion, enthusiasm, and dedication for what they do help them to create an aura of positivism around them. Regardless of any negativity that encompasses them, they produce a bubble of strength that enables them to continue. Sometimes this is through expressing their pain to others or by reflecting on their own personal strengths and weaknesses, by coming to know themselves better. They do not see themselves as caught in the stereotype of being "superwomen" but see themselves as real, acknowledging their strengths and weaknesses. Sometimes it is through their enthusiasm that simply squelches any negative energy present. Sometimes it is through making a conscious choice to be positive and to uphold important lifelong values regardless of the situation, thus extinguishing negative energy.

"Unfortunately there are folks who are threatened by my intelligence. I can read the signs that they are intimidated. What do I do? Well, I'm not going to play dumb, but I will perhaps, solicit their contributions," explains Amina.

Understanding and Affirmation of Their Own Values

The women hold strong convictions regarding their value system. They are unafraid to challenge individuals, policies, and institutions that conflict with their values. They are unafraid to question authority and challenge the status quo for an enhanced quality of life for all. They understand themselves in the context of their society with its positive and negative realities. They understand the cycle of oppression and its influence upon their and others' goals. Such understanding enables these women to direct their attention and efforts to what is important to counter oppressive situations. They are led by values that facilitate respect and dignity in all people and thus are able to take on challenges of oppression and injustice toward others. These are women who believe life and situations can always be better and work hard to ensure that it is, for themselves and for others. They love life and—knowing the importance of pleasure, joy, and relaxation in maintaining a balanced life—seek means to engage these important elements.

Cultivation of Outside Interests

Developing or maintaining interests and responsibilities outside of the university enables our participants to find value and affirmation in other areas when the going becomes tough in the academy. The women who do not permit academia to become their entire life seem to be happier. Tiye notes, "I get a lot of fulfillment outside the university from recreation, hobbies, and travel to participation—when I can—in community events. That seems to help me survive any negative stuff in academia." To be able to pull away and distance oneself from the negative drama allows one the space needed to regroup or to view the situation from a different perspective, resulting in more effective management of the issues.

Enthusiasm for Learning

The women talk passionately about the university as a place to explore and to express ideas. With a history of intellectual encouragement, the women find the university environment compatible with their need for intellectual expression. Engaging in conversations regarding issues of their profession, their society, the university, the world, and even oppression and systemic change are stimulating. Hearing others' perspectives and new ideas are welcomed. While they all find the university unwelcoming at times, they love the fact that it affords opportunities to engage in enriching dialogue on an ongoing basis. They speak of being intellectually well fed. They express hope for change in the academic environment as they engage in challenging discussions and explore new ideas. This is particularly noted by Tiye and Nandi, who mention that such enriching discussions seldom take place outside of the university among the people they are involved with in their communities.

Emotional Intelligence

When emotions get heated, being able to remain calm and view the issues from multiple perspectives is crucial. Also, being able to view the issues from the others' perspective, understanding their needs, and considering means of addressing them is more beneficial than continued argument. Nevertheless, when others are being disrespectful, arrogant, or unwilling to address alternatives, flying off the handle may be just the type of action that will really attract the necessary attention and force others to realize that the issues are real. In a sense, these women have learned to read their environment with a critical eye. Their experiences, research, and teaching enable them to become literate of the world landscape and its system of privilege; its system of aggression and oppression.

Spiritual Resources

Letting Go

The women acknowledge that they cannot do everything and often consider the implications of sometimes just letting go. They speak of times when they come to a quiet sense of peace and surrender to Divine power in order to manage difficult situations. Being competent and capable women, however, they note their struggle to do this but believe in the importance of letting go. For them, such surrender is difficult but is sometimes made.

Faith

There are frequently those times when one must rely upon spirit to bring about loving, compassionate actions. "Sometimes when things just aren't going well and I've done all that I know to do or have energy to do, I believe in the power of the Lord that things will work out for the best," states Cleopatra. During times of "letting go," the women hold a strong faith that justice will be served and that beneficial results will occur. While they acknowledge that life is not always fair, they rely on spirit to do the right thing. As long as they are doing the right thing, they believe spirit will come through.

Confronting Oppression

These women also have many opportunities to advocate, to speak out, and to demonstrate leadership in ways that challenge what is detrimental to others and to the development of their fullest potential. As difficult as their environment may be, having a voice against the issues provides a sense of empowerment for the women. They have an intense passion to face obstacles/challenges and to overcome them. They have learned to find alternative routes to reach their goals when obstacles block their paths. They regroup and strategize around the obstacles. They are willing to challenge and to change the system despite whatever personal fears or plans they may have. They stare the demon in the eye and refuse to blink. When beaten down, they simply regroup. They withstand the plummeting of the rain because they are grounded in the family and the cultural roots that love and sustain them. They find allies to support them in their challenge of the system. They have become keenly aware of the sociopolitical dynamics that maintain the status quo and oppress many groups of people.

The women are open and willing to acknowledge spirit as an aspect of their own accomplishments. They understand that their blessings come from divine power. They recognize a power higher than themselves in their life direction. They view their education, career, experiences, and life as a spiritual journey. Some of the women speak openly about their belief in God and their involvement in their churches. Others comment about the "spiritual power" they call upon to give them strength during stressful, troubled, and difficult times. Spiritual as well as humanistic values help these women to "keep on keepin' on" in spite of the obstacles. As Cleopatra says, "There is a greater reward."

Summary

The characteristics and coping mechanisms discussed have enabled the five women to achieve their dreams and to become successful in academia. Understanding the sociopolitical dynamics of the university as well as understanding and recognizing their own needs enable them to lay claim to their proper place in academia. The participants have acquired multiple resources for coping. Their coping strategies to succeed in academia are: enthusiasm for their profession; courage to challenge people and issues; commitment to high ideals of both humanity and spirit; professional and life dreams that extend beyond academia; possession of a deep understanding of their cultural heritage, the sociopolitical dynamics of the university, and oppression; an openness to collaboration; and a high level of self-efficacy. These coping mechanisms have developed from their strong family/community support, the validation of childhood experiences, and the continued reception of knowledge and experiences throughout their life journeys. They acknowledge the importance of using their resources collectively for the uplifting of all people, particularly African Americans and especially African American women, and so they attempt to mentor others in obtaining those characteristics necessary for survival and self-enhancement. These women hope to continue to utilize their resources, as we shall see.

CHAPTER 5
Nia
Expectations for the Future

Look full at life, right through to death. The future belongs to those who believe in the beauty of their dreams. (Eleanor Roosevelt)

There must be a purpose (nia) for African American women to invest so much of themselves into education and the academic setting in spite of the obstacles they encounter. While some people face challenges and eventually become disillusioned and give up, these women seem to have endless energy to keep going. To better understand what keeps them going, regardless of the challenges, let us turn now to the points in their stories where we catch a glimpse of their feelings and expectations for the future.

Cleopatra

Cleopatra, the dean, has a clear sense of who she is, what she wants to do, and what constitutes success for her. She knew very early in her life that she wanted to be in the field of education. She muses: "I knew as a child that I wanted to be a teacher. Playing school was my favorite pastime. I admired teachers and the way in which they had a positive impact on students. I wanted to be able to do that. I had many wonderful teachers who encouraged me along the way. I have been fortunate to be able to realize my dream, especially being in higher education for so many years. I have 'fallen' into a number of roles, all of which I've really enjoyed, and that, to me, constitutes success. I think that being able to make the choices you want to make, being in the environment you want to be in, and being in the profession you have chosen for life and really liking it is indeed a blessing. Most of all, I feel that I have been in a position to have a positive impact on colleagues and students. The most rewarding experiences I've had are conversations with former students and colleagues who said point blank: 'You've made a difference in my life. Thank you.' Now that's success."

Cleopatra currently sees herself in a stage of "wanderlust," desiring change and reaching out for other opportunities and challenges. She is generally satisfied with what she has accomplished and feels competent in her role. Her need for new challenges, however, causes her to consider positions both inside and outside of the university where she currently works. As an African American woman, Cleopatra feels that she has been able to assume her responsibilities and to move up the administrative ladder because she was well-prepared and was "in the right place at the right time."

Cleopatra is dedicated to helping all people and has a special, deep, and abiding commitment to helping people of color. "I want to help African American people because I know that in this society they face so many challenges." This desire is based in no small measure on her own personal experiences. She believes that her position as a dean is only valuable to the extent that she can help her own people in a significant way.

Whether in the university setting or elsewhere, Cleopatra desires to use her talents to uplift her people both intellectually and spiritually. Even her personal goals relate to providing a change that will impact others positively. Some of her personal goals include working in a predominantly Black institution as an administrator or faculty member and providing advice and counsel to people of color in creative and innovative ways.

Nandi

Nandi, the associate professor of business, also had a loving and nurturing childhood environment, much like her sisters. Many people around her have been supportive and have encouraged academics and discipline. This has undoubtedly contributed to her success as a student and as a professional.

Nandi views herself as a successful person in that she has been in positions where she can provide access for others. Her current goals are to establish a business and to go back into the inner city to work with youth. She has a strong commitment to assisting youth. Not only does she have the desire to help, but she knows she possesses the skills to benefit youth. Through this avenue, she knows she has purpose. Through her business she is hoping to not only positively impact youth, but to acquire economic enhancement that will place her in a position to financially support important issues. These, of course, would be issues related to the betterment of African Americans. "I believe that by assisting African Americans, all people are helped because the result would be fewer social ills for everyone. I don't mean this as a slam on African Americans. The fewer oppressive situations people have to encounter, the better off everyone is. Whenever anyone is helped and it results in fewer social ills, everyone benefits. However, my focus has always been on African Americans. Whatever impacts or influences one really impacts the whole. We are all interconnected."

The university setting has been one avenue for fulfilling her purpose. She now looks forward to establishing her business where she will have a center devoted to youth development. "I feel this is a calling from God. My desire is to impact hundreds of lives in a positive way. I have been blessed. I have a lot of energy, good health, and a lot of enthusiasm. This is really what I want to do. Everything that has happened in the past has led me to this. I know that God wants me to do this because so many roads have opened up for this to happen. I'm excited about this."

Nandi is committed to helping others, and when we hear her voice describing her dreams, we know that she demonstrates this commitment throughout life, regardless of the setting. "I am highly motivated and I like what I do," exclaims Nandi.

Nzingha

Nzingha, the law professor enjoys her work immensely and, like her other sisters, has overcome many obstacles to reach success in her chosen field. The desire to impact others' lives positively has been an important theme in the life of Nzingha. As Nzingha states, "Some would see the acquisition of full professorship as successful. Full professorship allows me the freedom, to some extent, to be left alone to do those things I define as meaningful. Doing what is meaningful is being successful. The kinds of things that are meaningful to me are those things that bring about something better than what was. If I can bring about a different curriculum, game, idea, book, or anything that would make things better for someone or a group of people, that is meaningful and thus successful."

While Nzingha acknowledges this life purpose, she also notes the difficulty of doing this. "For one, it is not an easy task to stay focused on what is meaningful. There are lots of what I call mundane activities or responsibilities that continue to compete for my time, even though as full professor I have a little more freedom than more junior faculty. Also, reaching this position as full professor has required me to do a lot of research, which has meant for me a lot of hours alone reading and writing and thinking. While I enjoy that, I miss being with people and at the grassroots of things. My publications I suppose help in reaching many people, professional people. But what I miss sometimes is the everyday contact with everyday folks with everyday issues. I'm not out there practicing law like I used to. Most of my work now consists of my research here at the university. I feel a need to get back out more into the community. I have to. That's where my life is. University life has been enriching and rewarding, but also a great sacrifice. I've sacrificed having close friendships because I've been so involved professionally." Nzingha hopes to reconnect with the community, potentially using her research to positively affect "everyday people."

Tiye

Tiye, the associate professor of counseling, states, "My work in academia has required a commuter lifestyle because the university I serve is located away from my residence and my husband maintains his job where we live. Although there are many aspects of academia I enjoy, I do not wish to continue the commuter lifestyle. It is too stressful. Since no university exists where I live, I will need to seek other employment opportunities or engage in activities that hopefully will afford me similar autonomy and leadership responsibilities. I desire to work toward helping others reach their potential and I enjoy bringing about systemic change that will benefit others, especially those who are usually taken advantage of. I desire to help others, especially African Americans, understand more about traditional African cosmology and its relationship to healing and living a healthy and satisfying life. I want others to know the richness of our African heritage and its value to current issues and wellness in a society that in many ways is so sick and where people have so little hope. I want to see our youth grow to feel confident about the richness of our culture and heritage. I want our people to know about the heart of African philosophy and people.

"I have traveled extensively and I have seen people living in all kinds of conditions, from the wealthy to those living in utter squalor. I have seen those who abuse their advantages and those who wish they had just a small piece of the pie. It breaks my heart knowing that there is so much suffering and knowing that many who have privileges take no action or don't care to reduce the suffering. Regardless, I want to continue to help, no matter where I may be located either professionally or socially."

The theme of success is summed up in Tiye's statement: "Success for me is measured by the impact I have upon others. Have I made a positive difference in the lives of others? Have I made a positive difference in policy or in social dynamics that contribute[s] to the enhancement or empowerment of others, particularly people of color? There is always work to do in that regard, so obtaining success is always in process. No one is ever completely there. Success is also completion of what I have started, goals I have established. When I finish an objective, for me that is success."

Tiye also shares that she loves the arts. "Success for me is also being able to express myself through the arts, whether it is dance, painting, playing music, or writing poetry. In this way I bring some measure of understanding and joy to others."

As Tiye studies nature and cares for her garden, she believes that all living things should have the opportunity to survive and reach their full potential. In other words, Tiye wants to continue helping others to reach their fullest potential.

"I am here for a purpose. I have been blessed with so many advantages. God has provided so much beauty all around us and I think humans keep messing it up. Nevertheless, God's beauty is all around us. I think I really want to write. I want to paint too. I love to paint. But I want my painting to express the beauty of God's world and the beauty of life. I want my paintings to speak to hope, love, beauty, health. I want my writings to do the same. In this way I hope to continue to contribute to the well-being of others."

Tiye also notes that she has grandchildren and wants to be involved in their lives in a positive and influential way. "My grandchildren are dear to me and I want the best for them, so I struggle a little between being involved in their lives and the professional things I still want to do. I know I can do them both, but I guess I want to integrate these two realities so that each benefits the other. Perhaps as I write and paint, I will teach my grandchildren and involve them in these activities."

Amina

Amina has a rich and demanding career in academia in the Black Studies Department. She, too, feels a strong obligation to be successful and to help others. Amina attributes that feeling to her ancestors who gave so much so that she could have the opportunity to carve out a career and to achieve her highest potential. It's what keeps her going. As Amina looks to the future she states: "I want to do more research and writing and go back to Ghana, which is my heart and soul. I love Ghana with a passion. I hope to teach there. I'd like to be involved in international affairs at some decision making, some policy level down the road where I can impact educational policy. I want to open doors for our next generation."

Amina's personal goals are clear: she wants to teach and to conduct research that leads to opening doors for future generations. Her purpose in life helps to keep her going despite the challenges she encounters.

Summary

What we notice immediately among these women is a sense of purpose that was certainly demonstrated in the university setting but that also goes far beyond the university. For these five women, their leadership positions in academia facilitate their journeys toward purpose and mission but are not their mission or purpose. A mission is not necessarily a profession or an occupation, but rather a "calling" or a "purpose for living." A mission is a spiritual message that links to one's reason for being created. Fulfilling a mission is therefore a spiritual journey. Coming to recognize their spiritual journey through the manifestation of purpose enables these women to stand their ground and to withstand obstacles they encounter.

Let us take a moment and view purpose (nia) from an Afrocentric perspective. As we understand purpose in this manner, we will see the significance of issues African American women in the academy face. The realization of purpose comes about through the community that acknowledges, approves, and confirms the individual's innate gifts. This spiritual journey is an unfolding of one's essence. These women experienced this confirmation in their childhood communities. The significant persons in the lives of these five women have assisted in creating their purpose. The community exists to safeguard the purpose of each person within it and to awaken the memory of that purpose by recognizing the unique gifts each individual brings to the world (Somé, 1998). Whether family or other groups of persons, the nature of community is extremely significant. These women have been awakened to their purpose through their respective communities, have listened to or have begun to listen to the whispers of their hearts, and are attuned to their passions. They have been encouraged to prepare for, to train for, to seek, and to discover their purpose. Healing comes when the individual remembers his or her purpose and reconnects with the world of spirit. Thus we all recognize at a deep level the importance for our own health and welfare of finding purpose.

However, purpose is not fulfilled without a price. As we have seen, purpose must be supported by community. A community of alienation where validation is absent often hinders or prevents the processes necessary for fulfilling purpose. Within the harsh reality of racial and sexual discrimination, where one's essence is devalued, fulfillment of purpose becomes a severe challenge. Feelings—such as avoidance, discomfort, rejection, and fear—may turn individuals away from their purpose. The abandonment of purpose, however, can result in a sense of despair, emptiness, and meaninglessness in life. Nevertheless, for these women the strong families and communities from which they come, coupled with their previous successes, assist them in overcoming alienation, rejection, and lack of validation as well as in reading their environment with a critical eye. Moving forward with purpose may be difficult, fearful, stressful, and lonely, but when individuals connect with their purpose, they are better able to live and to act with authentic effectiveness.

These women are not content with just fulfilling their job responsibilities at work because they know they have a greater existential purpose. Nandi captures this truth when she says, "My life is not my own. God has a purpose for me to encourage others and uplift them. The university is just one place in which I can fulfill that purpose." The women see their lives as fulfilling a greater purpose than the success of their careers. They talk about their passion and the inner voice that directs them. Tiye states, "God has a plan for me and sometimes I'm on the path and sometimes I'm not, but I know in my heart of the plan. When I'm not following His direction, I feel tense, but when I surrender myself to His direction, I feel spiritual peace and great accomplishment and satisfaction in what I am doing."

While some of the women state that they have often found themselves pulled in multiple directions, they seem to retain sight of why they have been created. They view their lives as being guided by spirit, feel great about what they have already accomplished, and acknowledge that there is more for them to do. Even though they encounter setbacks and various obstacles, including racism and sexism, they have not been hindered by these obstacles due to their greater motivation to fulfill their mission. They face difficulties, but they keep their purpose before them. They know that one must have long-range goals to keep from being frustrated by short-range failures.

These women are not content with the status quo. A recurring theme throughout their stories is the passionate desire to make a difference in the lives of others. The goals that they set for themselves speak clearly of their deep commitment to helping others to grow and to develop. Their passion is for assisting others and eradicating obstacles that interfere with others' growth and development. They grew up among those who had a commitment to bettering our society. This commitment is the glue that holds these sisters together. It is the core of their being. Indeed, it is their *raison d'être*. They have every intention to "keep on keepin' on" and to transfer the legacy of service to future generations. They know that their impact on a few lives helps all of humanity.

These women also welcome new challenges and opportunities in their professional and personal lives. When we look back into the family heritage of these women, they come from families that expected them to achieve and that instilled civic responsibility. These leading ladies are socially, politically, and racially conscious, as evidenced by their statements about helping students to grow, serving the community, staying in the "struggle" to combat racism and sexism, and developing themselves to be the best that they can be.

Mission enables these women to contextualize issues of race and gender. They are able to separate what is personal from what is contextual and to understand how social constructs can be internalized. These women know all too well the struggle of maintaining a sense of wholeness in an oppressive cultural environment. They have the experiences of being viewed as inferior or incompetent and of being treated with disrespect. They have struggled with resisting the internalization of oppression. "Sometimes when I face so much negativity, I get those feelings that I haven't accomplished much, that people don't care, that I'm not worth much. But then I have to choose to jump out of that mindset and to know that my support is God and that I am truly of value and what I am doing is good," confesses Tiye. They have dealt with their own feelings of anger and frustration stemming from oppressive acts. "Sometimes people act as if they don't like me simply because I'm intelligent. The rejection used to bother me, but now I realize that it's their problem," notes Nzingha. Nandi also speaks of the struggles with maintaining a happy family and meeting all the responsibilities of her professional life. "Balancing family and career is typically problematic for women. We have a lot of responsibility at home and at work." The women have been through the fire but have come out stronger. They have endured, manifesting a high self-esteem and sense of self-efficacy.

These are women who also know that their ancestors and their Creator support them as they strive toward their mission. They all speak of putting their trust in God regardless of what happens and believe that their ultimate purpose is to demonstrate God's love. "The greatest commandment is to love your neighbor as thyself and to love God with all your mind, body, and soul. When you think about it, that's a pretty tall order. I know I have failed to follow it at times, but I work on it. I know that helping others to be their best, giving encouragement, utilizing my talents for my pleasure and others' pleasure and benefit is all part of a greater plan. My demonstration of love to others is my ultimate purpose. God has blessed me with numerous avenues for doing so," affirms Nandi.

In the final analysis, the five women in our study have purpose (nia) that extends far beyond the university to the society and to life as a whole.

CHAPTER 6
Kuumba
Creating Change

If the human wealth could match the material wealth, what would happen? Heaven could be created, right here. (Malidoma Somé)

We have discussed the reality of academia in these women's lives, the strategies they utilize to cope within the context of academia, and their future expectations and purpose in academia and in life in general. In addition to the factors already mentioned in our results, we have noted two other aspects that these women either mention or imply as contributing to their success. This and the following chapter are devoted to these two components: creativity and faith, which are inextricably linked.

Creativity (kuumba) appears in our analysis. Statements that imply qualities of creativity center on trying something new and unconventional; being imaginative and curious; viewing situations from a different perspective; generating enthusiasm; attending to details, social patterns, and generalities that others don't seem to recognize; and taking advantage of opportunities to explore their environment.

From a humanist perspective, a social climate free from pressures for conformity and from stern evaluation is conducive to creativity. A basic adversary to creative impulses is an environment that inhibits the individual (Bloomberg, 1973). Flexible functioning, openness to new experiences, divergent thinking, and integration of remote associations are also related to creativity. Highly creative persons express novel ideas and stress their inventiveness, independence, individuality, enthusiasm, determination, and industry (Csikszentmihalyi, 1996; MacKinnon, 1961; Kersting, 2003). The women in our study exemplify these characteristics.

As we look at the childhood of the women in our study, we note that the five women were given the time, space, and security to explore their environment. They have had numerous opportunities to be open to information and to constantly changing data without preconceived or restricted interpretations of the world and their experiences. They were given the autonomy and freedom to be themselves and were encouraged to choreograph their own lives. Having few restrictions, being free from evaluation and stressful conditions, and being respected for their personhood, they were able to let their creative energies flow. We note that they also had opportunities for solitude in which they could engage in quiet reflection. Creativity requires intelligence and an analytic orientation in order to clarify, classify, and define details of problems, activities which can be engaged in during times of solitude.

Families and communities also help these women to acquire direction in their lives. They instill the women with motivation to carve out the direction they will take. The freedom they have experienced appears to have encouraged cognitive flexibility and an intrinsic motivation, both of which are related to creativity. Conditions such as time, space, autonomy, freedom, peace, solitude, security, reflection, intelligence, direction, and motivation are conducive to the implementation of creativity.

In the case of these women, creativity is, of course, couched in their desire to bring about change and to enrich the lives of others. Whether it is for their students, family, community, or profession, we see that each of the women is involved in activities to assist in the empowerment of others as well as of themselves. Even the very lives of these women serve as models of positive change. To bring about change requires creativity. Creativity involves stepping out of the norm, exploring, and considering the possibilities. The women in this study have always been excited by knowledge, new ideas, and new experiences. They take on the responsibility of creating change in their professions, societies, ethnic group, and families for the purpose of making life better. They are continually inspired to create new possibilities. Creativity often requires taking risks, meeting challenges, moving away from one's comfort zone, and being proactive. As we think about being proactive, we are reminded that a life lived by choice is a life of conscious action, while a life lived by chance is a life of unconscious <u>re</u>action. Thus when we are proactive, we take conscious action and we create. Proactive is the opposite of reactive.

Unfortunately, not all people think of their life journey as creative or believe that they possess the creativity necessary to bring about change. Creativity (kuumba) is not magical or foreign. Actually, we believe everyone has it, but too often individuals do not recognize or utilize their creativity, partly because they limit their notions of creativity to talents and skills they believe they do not possess and partly because they are too stressed or overwhelmed with life circumstances to develop their creativity. They may even think so poorly of themselves that they believe they cannot begin to imagine themselves as creative. The understanding of creativity as the bringing forth of new ideas, experiences, knowledge, and hope permits individuals to see creativity as something everyone possesses. The five women of this study are diligent users of their creative energy and capitalize upon their creative abilities because of conditions in their lives that foster their creativity.

As African American women, they come from a long tradition of creativity. Their African ancestors were the creators of language, writing, various forms of math, governments, science, medicine, calendars, buildings, and many other things. Their African American ancestors utilized many creative strategies during the period of enslavement to read, to write, to communicate in secret, and to escape bondage. For example, symbols in quilts, messages in songs, unique language forms and uses of words were creative methods of communicating needs, desires, and means of escaping. African Americans often utilized familiar and unassuming everyday items and materials—so as not to draw attention—for extraordinary purposes.

The African American women in our study utilize equally creative strategies to deal with the challenges they encounter in the university setting. Cleopatra speaks of how she uses her position as dean creatively to make a case, to articulate a vision, to network with others, and to provide resources for the benefit of students of color. Tiye speaks of the creativity she uses in establishing and implementing programs as well as in her teaching in order to open new worlds of knowledge and experience for others. Nandi, Tiye, and Nzingha utilize multiple methods of instruction—such as poetry, dance, songs, proverbs, drama, and sports—to relay information to students and colleagues. They also talk about how these strategies are often held in suspect by colleagues, some of whom view these methods as inferior. These women find themselves having to challenge this type of thinking. Amina is frustrated as she talks about the use of so much energy and time to prove her point or to justify her actions while many of her colleagues are already making headway up the professional ladder. Although Amina's inclination is to challenge prejudicial issues that arise, she sometimes creatively handles such difficult situations by demonstrating respect for others and by encouraging others' solutions.

In the university setting, these women often develop ways of helping with concerns such as tenure and promotion. They speak of assisting in the formation of coalitions to work the system to their advantage. Usually they do so quietly but at the same time give strong voice to concerns that impact people of color. They often engage others' participation and input in order to help give voice to prejudicial issues that arise. They encounter barriers but use imagination and innovation to overcome them.

Self-determination and confidence are important in implementing one's creative power. Creating carries the burden of trying new dance steps and being different from those around you. These women are sometimes misunderstood and suffer mistreatment because they dare to be different. How is it that they do not succumb to the peer pressures of conformity? Although they explain experiences of rejection and are said to be thought of as strange, weird, or simply different, they continue to function according to their purposes and values. They are motivated by their strong purposes, values, and missions. Their missions become their guides for behavior regardless of what rejection they may experience. Furthermore, they are not inclined to give up on their missions; rather, they were raised to believe that they are entitled to all possibilities. The word "can't" is not a familiar reality in their lives. Being free to be different requires an attitude of entitlement, a belief that what one strives for is already theirs. They know that they only have to put forth the energy and to utilize their creativity to obtain their desires.

Obstacles have been frequent in the women's lives because they are on a journey. If one has no journey, there are no obstacles to encounter. The one who risks the journey will encounter numerous challenges. In academia, the women are creative in their ability to manage the inhospitable environments in which they often find themselves. Sometimes it means remaining quiet. Sometimes it means confronting the situation head-on. Sometimes it means taking an alternative path to the same goal. The women utilize creativity to work around or through oppression and obstacles. For example, knowing that some of her colleagues viewed her as deficiently skilled and undependable, Tiye developed a program that earned her colleagues' high esteem and respect.

We notice that these women engage in continual, critical self-examination and strive to utilize their resources to create a positive sense of self. They continually create who they wish to be. As they critically examine themselves, they are recreating themselves in the image of their highest idea about who they can be. They are keenly aware of their strengths and their weaknesses and work hard to capitalize upon their strengths and to reduce the effects of their weaknesses. These women are not inclined to be boxed in by stereotypes, economics, and other conditions that would prevent them from choreographing their own special path in life. They talk about each day as a fresh beginning for directing their steps to meeting current challenges. As these women become stronger in their own identities, they are in the process of more intentionally expressing and demonstrating their own essence.

With such a perspective ingrained into these women's hearts, they believe they can create and recreate their own life journeys and fulfill their missions regardless of what others say or do. Dr. Martin Luther King, Jr. once stated, "Forces that threaten to negate life must be challenged by courage, which is the power of life to affirm itself in spite of life's ambiguities. This requires the exercise of a creative will that enables us to hew out a stone of hope from a mountain of despair." It is this creative will that enables the women to meet each day with renewed energy and determination, to experience life to its fullest, and to realize the best in others and themselves. It is this creative will that enables the women to seek and to explore new and different ways of fulfilling their missions. These are not women inclined to follow the crowd. Too often, as Dr. King stated, "People are like thermometers that record or register the temperature of majority opinion." These women are phenomenal in that they have chosen paths of risk and challenge and persevere despite their fears and obstacles. These women are not thermometers, but more like, quoting Dr. King, thermostats that transform and regulate the temperature of society.

CHAPTER 7
Imani
Recommendations for a Different Tomorrow

Now faith is the substance of things hoped for, the evidence of things not seen. (Hebrew 11:1)

In this chapter we discuss the second of the two components mentioned in the previous chapter, namely, faith. While the concept of faith is difficult to capture through research, we have distilled this concept from the women's previous comments. Faith serves as a culminating core that fuses everything else together. The women's faith is a thread running through their lives. Nandi makes this clear when she explains what got her through the difficult times: "When I think of all the struggles and uncertainties I've been through ... to be where I am now ... it was through my belief in God and only by the grace of God."

As the women talk about both their accomplishments and their struggles, we recognize an internal drive and spirit within each of them that directs and leads them to take action. We note that they are extremely optimistic and possess a belief that things will turn out for the best, regardless of initial setbacks. They believe that persistence is a key factor in achieving favorable results. Whereas some people abandon their efforts and beliefs, these women persist until they reach their dreams. "It's all about persistence and faith," notes Tiye.

Faith is the belief that hopes will become real, that things will happen in one's best interest. Those with faith hold the belief that people can achieve and sustain themselves against the odds when they employ their talents, intellect, and skills for the enhancement of others. They believe that by doing the "right thing," things will turn out for the best.

Each of the women speaks of the faith modeled by her family. "When things seemed impossible, Mom would get on her knees ... or sometimes she would just fold her hands and bow her head. I knew she was praying. After her prayers, somehow things would just turn out okay," recalls Nzingha. These five phenomenal women have been encouraged by their families to utilize their strengths, to acknowledge their limitations, and to rely on divine power. Internalizing their families' belief systems, these women believe that if they capitalize upon their talents, intellect, and skills, external factors will eventually align with their objectives, goals, and purpose. They also rely upon a higher power when situations arise where they have no power to affect change.

We learn from these women that faith is built over time. Not only has faith been modeled in their families, it has grown through seeing their own dreams come to fruition. As each prayer is answered, their faith becomes stronger. We also know, however, that not all prayers are answered affirmatively since people do not always get what they want and hope for. When hopes are shattered, suddenly life seems unfair. Yet, with a background of answered prayers, with a storage house full of talents and skills, with a host of people who believe in them, these women did not give up in the face of a setback. They assume the setback or unanswered prayer is part of an even greater purpose. Nandi puts it so well when she says, "Prayer is not about what I want but how I can best serve the Lord and trying to do that regardless of the situation I am in. I just have to have faith that He knows best, no matter the situation."

When Tiye did not obtain a counseling job for which she applied, she states, "I was very disappointed ... even a bit angry, but somehow I knew that something better would come along. And it eventually did. As I look back now, the opportunities that opened up for me as a result of not getting that particular job were wonderful. I could not have planned it better. God knew what He was doing." Cleopatra recalls a similar experience when she was not able to secure an appointment that suited her well. Although it was a great disappointment, over time she realized that she has a greater opportunity in the position she currently occupies. She also learns and grows from such experiences. Cleopatra has learned a lot about institutional racism and has developed a thicker skin to deal with such "vicious racism." Despite this experience, faith has been restored and she maintains her confidence.

Such experiences enable these women to rely on faith and to grow stronger in their faith. When they do not understand why things happen as they do—when they are filled with disappointment, fear, and uncertainty—they rely on the hope that things will turn out better in the future, and things usually do. As Tiye says, "It's hard sometimes when prayers aren't answered, but I've learned to rely completely on God and to demonstrate love everywhere I go regardless of whether my prayer was answered. I remember my grandmother saying, 'In <u>everything</u> give thanks to God.' That's hard at times, but I do try to use that philosophy." When situations do not work out as they hope, the women speak of maintaining and regaining faith, of believing that what will result will be for the best. They also speak of learning more about themselves and of finding that they relate to others more effectively. As a result of such experiences, the women note that they continue to learn how to release control. This often proves difficult for such accomplished individuals; however they are learning to balance their need and desire for power and control with their faith that things will turn out fine in the long run.

Amina speaks emotionally of the time she had hoped for a wonderful family and for a leadership role in her profession. When the reality of divorce smacked her in the face and career conflicts hindered her implementation of positive ideas and strategies, she was devastated. Everything seemed to be out of her control. Yet with courage, support from her family and friends, and reliance upon her faith that everything will be fine, she waited patiently, endured the pain, and then began to strategize for a different future. Change took time, but the results have benefited Amina.

The women believe in themselves because they have undergone successful experiences. They believe in themselves because they have faith that their mission is a spiritual undertaking. They believe in themselves because they have purpose and know they are entitled to it by spirit. They are excited about life, with all its challenges, because they are open to new knowledge that they can incorporate into their journeys. The women often seek to help others, knowing full well that they will not be compensated for their extra work. They are not seeking to serve others for the sake of making a profit, but simply to serve others, which sometimes profits them. The women speak of their many unexpected blessings that seem to make no sense but happen anyway. They even speak of blessings that they feel they do not deserve. They attest that they can only stand in awe at God's reasoning.

The women have each faced numerous situations where it seemed impossible to achieve what they have. Nevertheless, they proceed as if they know they are going to make it. Cleopatra had no idea how she was going to attend college; she certainly saw her chances for continuing with her education drying up as her family situation changed. Nandi had no financial resources for going to graduate school. Amina wondered whether she would ever get through the educational process after being discredited by so many teachers. Nevertheless, they have accomplished what, at the time, appeared nearly impossible. As they have continued in life, other opportunities have opened for them, and they gain strength and confidence that divine power is working with them.

Most importantly, the women speak of acting based upon a higher sense of values, of transcending the mundane, and of being led by a spiritual core deep within their persons. They have learned to welcome each day as a new beginning with numerous opportunities and possibilities. They continue to meet each day with optimism. Tiye affirms this observation when she says: "When I went up for promotion and tenure, I knew it would happen. The notion that I would not obtain it never crossed my mind. When I was hired, the idea that I would be rejected never entered my soul. I just knew, deep inside, it would happen." Optimism is really your self-fulfilling prophecy (Patterson-Stewart, 2001). As Dr. Patterson-Stewart observed, "Have you noticed, that after the rainstorm the bee goes back to the flowers; after the storm, the flower opens and stands tall again; creatures and plants expect the best from nature. We must do the same."

Summary

These women acknowledge the creativity, hard work, and faith that it will take to make a change in academia. For a more conducive environment in academia, minds will need to collectively recreate the academic environment. As this study affirms, academic institutions must take steps to help create a more hospitable environment in order to retain African American women. It is important for African American faculty and administrators, together with other leaders in the academic community, to come together to make recommendations specific to their settings.

Based on what has been gleaned from the voices of the women in this study, we would like to make a number of recommendations for African American women who take responsibility for their direction and are guided by what is truly within them. These recommendations manifest the values and principles demonstrated by these successful women. The principles that we must uphold and by which we live and gain success we view through the seven principles of the Nguzo Saba as articulated by Dr. Maulana Karenga. The seven principles are unity—umoja; self-determination—kujichagulia; collective work and responsibility—ujima; cooperative economics—ujamaa; purpose—nia; creativity—kuumba; and faith—imani. In terms of applying these principles to academia, we, as the authors, borrow from work initiated by Dr. Fran Dorsey (1990), *A Rhetoric of Values: An Afrocentric Analysis of Marcus Garvey's Convention Speeches, 1921-24*, and from *The Seven Principles in Higher Education*, written by Dr. Fran Dorsey and Dr. Marlene Dorsey.

Umoja—Unity

A strong network of support among the African Americans on campus can be formed. These should be well established and unified communities or organizations that provide information necessary for success and for challenging racism, sexism, and other oppressive activities. A solid network can help to alleviate the isolation that many African American women experience as the "lone Black" in the department. Unified as a community, African Americans have a more powerful voice with which to challenge the structure of entrenched arrangements such as unfair, biased, or unbalanced hiring, retention, tenure, and promotion practices. African American faculty and administrators encountering critical student and peer evaluations can benefit from a unified community that provides constructive feedback for professional development. Such a community can help junior faculty and administrators to address performance evaluations based on evidence as opposed to assumptions. A group or organization that addresses such concerns provides a forum through which African American women can obtain reality checks to their experiences of bias and prejudice. It will aid them in sorting out what is really happening to them and why they feel as they do. A supportive network that faculty and administrators can rely upon when issues arise can help to reduce frustration, uncertainty, and confusion about handling such issues.

Establishing a strong network among African Americans may be a difficult task. Ridding ourselves of indoctrinated individualism, competitiveness, and jealousy may be necessary. Also, campuses with few African Americans may find it necessary to establish or utilize community organizations. Nevertheless, as noted throughout the expressions of the five women in this study, to survive and to be successful in academia, unity (umoja) is extremely important.

Kujichagulia—Self-Determination

Self-determination has assisted the five women in our study to reach their goals within academia and is an important factor in facilitating their continued success. However, our study participants speak of being pulled in numerous directions. Because African American women are not typically valued as researchers, they are far too frequently expected to serve on numerous committees as well as to advise, to teach, and to mentor unreasonable numbers of students. This overloading hinders their research objectives. As a result, their path toward tenure and promotion is often compromised. In addition, African American women's desire to serve as caretakers for youth and to fight for the causes of their racial group often results in internal pressures leading to role overload. While their ultimate purpose may be to benefit students, to fight oppression, and to enhance their profession and life, African American women can benefit from mentoring that helps them to define their own path and direction within the academy, enabling them to narrow their altruistic desires and to focus on academic and professional pursuits that will facilitate their success. In this way they can more effectively implement their professional and altruistic life goals later, reducing the constant pull in multiple directions that does not benefit them or help them to achieve their goals. It is important that they set a research agenda early and define specifically how they want their career to proceed. Being passionate about their professional goals can help drive the tenure process and their career. They should initiate discussions with their dean and department chair to obtain specific information regarding expectations for tenure and promotion. Understanding that they do not have to do and to be everything <u>now</u> can be beneficial and can assist them in reducing the current load, helping them to establish long term goals.

Historically the academy has not valued research on issues facing African Americans, although this has been changing in recent years. Too often African Americans confront negative stereotypes developed and sanctioned by White scholars. The community of scholars, faculty, and administrators must work diligently against this negative portrayal. African Americans must take charge of the research that focuses on them. They must define and promote their own positive image. They must not only take charge of recreating and valuing themselves through research, but they must also support research through the sharing of strategies for effective research and writing, through access to funding resources, and through purchase and utilization of the fruits of such research.

Ujima—Collective Work and Responsibility

African American women must work together across disciplinary lines whenever possible. They can support the work of others who are conducting research on African Americans and on other people of color. This also means supporting existing academic research and cultural programs on campuses. Through the practice of ujima, African American women can more effectively demonstrate the value of research on African American issues. When working alone, it is easier for the general population of faculty and administrators to ignore such research. However, imagine the impact and power that can be illustrated when groups of African Americans come together to engage in an area of research. They can also emphasize the value and importance of such research by obtaining the involvement and participation of non-African Americans in their research. While not all research by African Americans must be focused on African American issues, they can model excellence in research skills no matter the topic and can, through ujima, advance more rapidly and effectively.

Ujamaa—Cooperative Economics

Economics is defined here as African American human resources—the Black pool of talent and Black capital available in the academy. It is important to use this pool of African American talent to write, to conduct research, and to produce creative works that define, support, and uplift who and what we are as African people. Intellectual talent is a resource. The women in this study certainly represent a pool of intellectual talent. For far too long, the military did not utilize its African American soldiers in combat. For far too long, the NBA did not utilize African American basketball players. For far too long, the Nurses Association did not utilize African American nurses in hospitals. This neglect of human resources should not occur in academia where intellectual talent is a highly prized commodity. African American women have much to offer as faculty and administrators. The university must challenge its negative perception of African American intellect and create an environment where this resource is viewed and utilized as an invaluable asset.

Ujamaa means supporting African Americans by buying the books of African American colleagues and attending their presentations. It is believed that if we are going to control our own destinies, we must establish our own plan and fund our own struggle (Reid-Merritt, 1996; Smiley, 2006). Bessie House-Soremekun (2002) stated that "Economic empowerment is one of the most critical problems facing the African American community today" (p. xxi). The potential for entrepreneurship in the realm of research and other intellectual pursuits can be very rewarding.

Nia—Purpose

As African American women in PWIs, we have a special purpose beyond teaching, research, and administrative and service responsibilities. African American faculty and administrators serve as role models for students of color on the campus. They can inspire and provide hope for many students to excel through their demonstration of professionalism. A common theme among the women in the study is their desire to help the next generation to lead the nation, to reduce further exploitation of people, and to encourage others in the creation of a transformative pedagogy. Assisting students of color to achieve their goals and objectives serves the ultimate purpose of the "liberation of Black people." This is a significant responsibility in the African American community. Indeed, these women definitely aid this purpose.

In addition, the university must be purposeful in its intent to retain African American faculty and administrators. The university's departments and programs can provide detailed and specific information regarding tenure and promotion that will benefit African American women. The university can refrain from its expectation that African American women serve as the voice of African Americans on numerous committees and as mentor and advisor of students of color. African American women must also be purposeful in their intent to succeed. This means carefully attending to their professional and personal development by continually updating themselves, exhibiting professionalism at all times, and staying focused on their goals.

Kuumba—Creativity

Creativity abounds among African American women in the academy. The talent that they bring to the academy, however, is often viewed as less than or inferior to that of their White colleagues, as the women in the study show. Institutional leadership must continue to challenge their academic departments to develop more creative approaches to utilize, to affirm, and to evaluate the talent of African American women. Competitive structures discourage change and diversity. Cooperation, however, promotes mutual goals and positive relationships that honor and respect diverse needs, interests, and methods of functioning (Lee, 2004). An environment that encourages the freedom to utilize all their creativity can facilitate the success of African American women, allowing them to bring their unique talents to teaching and research, thereby enriching academic programs.

Imani—Faith

As many of the women attest, "We've come this far by faith." Certainly strong spiritual values are important, being coupled with hard work and tenacity. African American women are fortunate to have, on some campuses, programs and services that affirm their cultural identity and uplift them spiritually. University leaders can work together to promote such programs and services, providing opportunities where strength and faith can be renewed, particularly during troubled times on campus. Such safe havens are vital, as they reflect the qualities and values of the early childhood development of the participants. They must be protected by any means necessary.

BIBLIOGRAPHY

Aguirre, A. (2000). *Women and minority faculty in the academic workplace: Recruitment, retention, and academic culture.* Washington, DC: ERIC Clearinghouse on Higher Education, ERIC Digests. (ERIC Document Reproduction Service No. ED446723.)

Akbar, N. (1984). *Chains and images of psychological slavery.* Jersey City, NJ: New Mind Productions.

Alfred, M. (2001). Reconceptualizing marginality from the margins: Perspectives of African American tenured female faculty at a White research university. *The Western Journal of Black Studies, 25*, 1–11.

Antonio, A. L. (2002). Faculty of color reconsidered: Reassessing contributions to scholarship. *Journal of Higher Education, 73*, 582–603.

Bennett, J. B. (1998). *Collegial professionalism: The academy, individualism and the common good.* American Council on Education and the Oryx Press.

Bjorck, J. P.; and Cohen, L. H. (1993). Coping with threats, losses, and challenges. *Journal of Social and Clinical Psychology, 12*, 36–72.

Blackwell, J. (1983). *Networking and mentoring: A study of cross-generational experiences of Black graduate and professional schools.* Atlanta, GA: Southern Education Foundation.

Bloomberg, M. (1973). *Creativity: Theory and research.* New Haven, Connecticut: College and University Press.

Boyd, J. (1993). *In the company of my sisters.* New York, N.Y.: Penguin Books.

Bradley, C.; and Holcomb-McCoy, C. (2004). African American counselor educators: Their experiences, challenges, and recommendations. *Counselor Education and Supervision, 43,* 258–273.

Brown, S. (1988). *Increasing minority faculty: An elusive goal.* Princeton, N. J.: Educational Testing Service.

Bryant, R. M.; Coker, A. D.; Durodoye, B. A.; McCollum, V. J.; Pack-Brown, S. P.; Constantine, M. G.; O'Bryant, B. J. (2005). Having our say: African American women, diversity, and counseling. *Journal of Counseling and Development, 83,* 313–319.

Budweiser Company. (1995). *The 20th anniversary, Budweiser: Great kings and queens of Africa.* Budweiser Company.

Ceridian.com/myceridian/connection/content/1,40268,13758-61510,00.html (2006, June). *The beauty bias: Physical attractiveness and the hiring process.* Ceridian Connection: A monthly newsletter.

Clarke, J. H. (1992). African warrior queens. In I. Van Sertima (Ed.). *Black women in antiquity* (pp. 123–134). New Brunswick: Transaction Publishers.

Coker, A. D. (2003, February). *African American women and the utilization of counseling services.* Paper presented at the American Association of Behavioral and Social Sciences sixth annual meeting. Las Vegas, NV.

Cooper, T. L. (2006). *The sista' network: African American women faculty successfully negotiating the road to tenure.* Bolton, MA: Anker Publishing Co.

Csikszentmihalyi, M. (1996). *Creativity: Flow and the psychology of discovery and invention.* New York, N.Y.: Harper Collins Publishers.

Davis, A. (1983). *Women, race and class.* New York: Random House.

Davis, L. (1985). Black and White social work faculty: Perceptions of respect, satisfaction, and job permanence. *Journal of Sociology and Social Welfare, 12,* 79–94.

DeFour, D. and Hirsch, B. (1990). The adaptation of Black graduate students: A social network approach. *American Journal of Community Psychology, 18,* 487–503.

Dipboye, R. L.; Arvey, R. D.; and Terpstra, D. E. (1977). Sex and physical attractiveness of raters and applicants as determinants of resume evaluations. *Journal of Applied Psychology, 62,* 288–294.

Dorsey, F. (1990). *A Rhetoric of Values: An Afrocentric Analysis of Marcus Garvey's Convention Speeches, 1921–24.* Unpublished doctoral dissertation. Kent State University, Kent, OH.

Drummond, E. H. (1997). *Overcoming anxiety without tranquilizers.* New York: Penguin Books.

Edwards, J. and Camblin, L. (1998). Assorted adaptations by African American administrators. *Women in Higher Education, 7(11)*, 33.

English, R. (1984). *The challenge for mental health: Minorities and their world views.* Proceedings of the 2nd Annual Robert Sutherland Lecture, University of Texas, Austin TX, Hogg Foundation for Mental Health, Publications Division.

Etter-Lewis, G. (1993). *My soul is my own: Oral narratives of African American women in the professions.* New York: Routledge.

Friere, P. (2001). Pedagogy of the oppressed (M.B. Ramos, Trans.). New York: Continuum. (Original work published 1970).

Graves, S. B. (1990). A case of double jeopardy? Black women in higher education. *Initiatives, 53*, 3–8.

Gregory, S.T. (1995). *Black women in the academy: The secrets to success and achievement.* New York: University Press of America, Inc.

Gregory, S. T. (2001). Black faculty women in the academy: History, status and future. *Journal of Negro Education, 70*, 124-139.

Grier, W. H. and Cobbs, P. M. (1992). *Black rage.* New York: Basic Books.

Hanson, S.; Martin, J. K.; and Tuch, S. A. (1987). Economic sector and job satisfaction. *Work and Occupation, 14*: 286–305.

Hathaway, W. L. and Pargament, K. L. (1992). The religious dimensions of coping: Implications for prevention and promotion. In K.I. Pargament, K. I. Maton, and R. E. Hess (Eds.), *Religion and prevention in mental health: Research, vision and action* (pp. 129–154). New York: Haworth Press.

Herzberg, F. (1972). *Work and the nature of man.* New York: World Publishing.

House-Soremekun, B. (2002). *Confronting the odds: African American entrepreneurship in Cleveland, Ohio.* Kent, Ohio: Kent State University Press.

Hudson-Weems, C. (1989). The tripartite plight of African American women as reflected in the novels of Hurston and Walker. *Journal of Black Studies, 20*, 192–207.

Jackson, A. and Sears, S. (1992). Implications of an Africentric world view in reducing stress for African American women. *Journal of Counseling and Development, 71(2)*, 184–190.

James, J. and Farmer, R. (Eds.). (1993). *Spirit, space and survival: African American women in (White) academia*. New York: Routledge.

Josephs, R.A.; Markus, H.R.; and Tafarodi, R. W. (1992). Gender and self-esteem. *Journal of Personality and Social Psychology, 63*, 391–402.

Karenga, M. (1998). *Kwanzaa: A celebration of family, community, and culture, commemorative edition*. Los Angeles: University of Sankore.

Kersting, K. (2003). Consider creativity: What exactly is creativity? *APA Monitor on Psychology, 34(10)*, 40–41.

Lee, V. V. (2004). Violence-prevention and conflict-resolution education in the schools. In R. Perusse and G. E. Goodnough (Eds.). *Leadership, advocacy, and direct service strategies for professional school counselors*. Belmont, CA: Brooks/Cole-Thomson Learning.

Lipford-Sanders, J. and Bradley, C. (2005). Multiple-lens paradigm: Evaluating African American girls and their development. *Journal of Counseling and Development, 83*, 299-304.

MacKinnon, D. W. (1961). The study of creativity and creativity in architects. In, *Conference on the creative person*. Berkeley: University of California, Institute of Personality Assessment and Research. Ch. 1 and 5.

Malveaux, J. (1984, April). Black women and stress. Essence, 74–76, 151–152, 154.

Marshall, C. and Rossman, G. (1999). Designing qualitative research (3rd ed.). Thousand Oaks, CA: Sage.

Maruyama, M. (1978). Psychotopology and its applications to cross-disciplinary, cross-professional, and cross-cultural communication. In R.E. Hollomon and S.A. Arutiunov (Eds.), *Perspectives on Ethnicity* (pp. 23–75). The Hague: Mouton.

McCray, C. (1980). The Black woman and family roles. In LaFrances Rodgers-Rose (Ed.), *The Black woman* (pp. 67–78). Beverly Hills: Sage Publications.

Miles, M. and Huberman, A. (1994). *Qualitative data analysis.* Beverly Hills, CA: Sage.

Moses, Y. (1989, August). *Black women in academia: Issues and strategies.* Baltimore: Project on the Status of Education of Women.

Patterson-Stewart, K. (2001). *Seven blessings from a pink slip.* Toledo, OH: PSC Services, Ltd.

Patton, M. Q. (1990). *Qualitative evaluation and research methods.* London: Sage.

Peterson, S, (1990). Challenges for black women faculty. *Initiatives, 53*(1), 33-36.

Reid-Merritt, P. (1996). *Sister power: How phenomenal Black women are rising to the top.* New York: John Wiley and Sons, Inc.

Reskin, B. and Phipps, P. (1988). Women in male-dominated professional and managerial occupations. In A. H. Stromberg and S. Harkess (Ed.), *Working women: Theories and facts in perspective* (pp. 190–205). Palo Alto, CA: Mayfield Publishers.

Robertson, L. J. and Bean, J. P. (1998). Women faculty in family and consumer sciences: Influences on job satisfaction. *Family and Consumer Sciences Research Journal, 27,* 167–194.

Rodgers-Rose, L. and Rodgers, J. (1985). *Strategies for resolving conflict in Black male and female relationships.* Newark, NJ: Traces Institute Publications.

Rothenberg, P. S. (1998). *Race, class, and gender in the United States: An integrated study* (Fourth Edition). New York: St. Martin's Press.

Shahani-Denning, C. (2003). *Physical attractiveness bias in hiring: What is beautiful is good*. Department of Psychology, Hofstra University.

Simms, M. and Malveaux, J. (Eds.) (1986). *Slipping through the cracks: The status of Black women*. New Brunswick: Transaction Books.

Skolnick, A. S. (1986). *The psychology of human development*. Sand Diego: Harcourt Brace.

Smiley, T. (2006). *The covenant with Black America*. Chicago: Third World Press.

Smith, E. (1992). *A comparative study of occupational stress in African American and White university faculty*. New York: Edwin Mellen Press.

Smith, D.; Wolf, L. E.; and Busenberg, B. E. (1996). *Achieving faculty diversity: Debunking the myths*. Washington, DC: Association of American Colleges and Universities.

Snyder, T. (1987). *Digest of educational statistics*. Washington, D. C.: Department of Education.

Somé, M. P. (1998). *The healing wisdom of Africa: Finding life purpose through nature, ritual, and community*. New York: Penquin Putnam.

Spottswood-Simon, V. (1992). Tiye: Nubian queen of Egypt. In I. Van Sertima (Ed.). *Black women in antiquity* (pp. 56–63). New Brunswick: Transaction Publishers.

St. John, E. (2000). More doctorates in the house. *Black Issues in Higher Education, 17*, 10–38.

Staples, R. and Johnson, L. B. (1995). *Black families at the crossroads: Challenges and prospects*. San Francisco, CA: Jossey-Bass.

Strauss, A. and Corbin, J. (1990). *Basics of qualitative research: Grounded theory procedures and techniques.* Newbury Park: SAGE Publications, Inc.

Thomas, G. (1981). *Black students in higher education.* Westport, CT: Greenwood Press.

Thomas, G. and Hollenshead, C. (2001). Resisting from the margins: The coping strategies of Black women and the other women of color faculty members at a research university. *Journal of Negro Education, 70,* 166–176.

Turner, S. V. (2002). Women of color in academe: Living with multiple marginality. *Journal of Higher Education, 73,* 74–94.

Turner, S. V. and Myers, S. L. (2000). *Faculty of color in academe: Bittersweet success.* Needham Heights, MA: Allyn and Bacon.

Turner, S. V.; Myers, S. L.; and Creswell, T. (1999). Exploring underrepresentation: The case of faculty of color in the Midwest. *Journal of Higher Education, 70,* 3–27.

Vaughn, D.C. (1986). Stress and the American Black woman: Analysis of research. *International Journal for the Advancement of Counseling, 9,* 341–350.

Viewzone.com (2005, Fall). *Undeniable bias toward the beautiful.* Emerge Newsletter, 2(3). Hofstra University.

West, C. (1993). *Race matters.* New York: Vintage Books.

West, C. M. (1995). Mammy, Sapphire, and Jezebel: Historical images of Black women and their implications for psychotherapy. *Psychotherapy, 32,* 458–466.

White, D. G. (1999). *Ar'n't I a woman?: Female slaves in the plantation South* (Rev. ed.). New York: Norton.

Williams, C. B. (2005). Counseling African American women: Multiple identities—multiple constraints. *Journal of Counseling and Development, 83*, 278–283.

Williams, D. R. (2001). Racial variations in adult health status: Patterns, paradoxes, and prospects. In N. J. Smelser, W. J. Wilson, and F. Mitchell (Eds.), *America becoming: Racial trends and their consequences* (pp. 371–410). Washington, DC: National Academyn Press.

Williams, M. S.; Jerome, A.; White, K.; and Fisher, A. (2006). Making sense of suffering: A preliminary study of changes in religious women adjusting to severe adversity. *Counseling and Values, 50*, 84–98.

World Book Encyclopedia. (1976). *Cleopatra. Vol. 4.* Chicago: Field Enterprises Educational Corporation.

Young, C. (1989). Psychodynamics of coping and survival of the African-American female in a changing world. *Journal of Black Studies, 20(2),* 208–223.

ANITA P. JACKSON is a native of Cleveland, Ohio. She received her Ph.D. in Counselor Education from The Ohio State University in 1989. She is Emeritus Professor in Counseling and Human Development of the College and Graduate School of Education, Health, and Human Services at Kent State University. She is also a practicing Clinical Counselor and Supervisor at Muskingum Valley Health Center in Zanesville, Ohio. Her research interests include HIV/AIDS prevention, stress, and multicultural counseling and women's issues. Her research publications focus on these topics as well as African American development.

MARLENE R. DORSEY, born in Pittsburgh, PA, is a long time resident of Cleveland, Ohio. She received her Ph.D. in Educational Administration from Kent State University in 1980. She is recently retired from her position as Dean of the College of Continuing Studies and Associate Professor of Higher Education Administration in the College and Graduate School of Education, Health, and Human Services at Kent State University. Her research interests include retention, diversity, and leadership issues in higher education.

LaVergne, TN USA
02 November 2009
162829LV00003B/63/P